-The timeless attitude that attract great guys to your life.-

BECOMING THE LADY GUYS ARE EAGER TO MARRY.

HOW TO GET MARRIED - FASTER THAN YOU EVER THOUGHT POSSIBLE

FESTUS A TOKS

iUniverse, Inc.

New York   Bloomington

BECOMING THE LADY GUYS
ARE EAGER TO MARRY
How To Get Married Faster Than
You Ever Thought Possible

iUniverse books may be ordered through booksellers or by contacting:

iUniverse
1663 Liberty Drive
Bloomington, IN 47403
www.iuniverse.com
1-800-Authors (1-800-288-4677)

ISBN: 978-1-4401-1290-4 (pbk)
ISBN: 978-1-4401-2365-8 (ebk)

Printed in the United States of America

iUniverse rev. date: 12/29/2008

CONTENTS

DEDICATION;

First and foremost, I want to dedicate this unique book to the Almighty God for the wonderful and excellent wisdom, knowledge and insights bestowed on me.

The book is also dedicated to my loving mother, Mrs Felicia Akinsiku for her wonderful and immeasurable love, care, and commitment to my course in life.

Also to my Sisters; Omowunmi, Aarinade, Yinka, Bunmi and Mercy for being a wonderful companions and loving relations.

Also to my female friends, Becky, Oke, Rita, Poweide, Amina, Ronke, Gloria, Abimbola, Angela, Rosemary, and Ufuoma for our wonderful relationships over the years. I have learnt great lessons from you all

And to the billions of the 21st Century Ladies; this is my unique gift to you all.

ACKNOWLEDGMENT

It is only a teamwork that makes the dream work. This unique work would not have been a success without the help and assistance of some remarkable and excellent people which include

Mr Anuoluwapo Odusami; an Information Technology Consultant at Lexium Technologies, Lagos, Nigeria

Also to my editor; Mr Chris Sage Ofojebe.
        E-mail: Krizsage@yahoo.com
        08037113856.0
        www.geocities.com/krizsage/sage.html

Special thanks to my spiritual fathers, teachers and mentors; Pastor E.A Adeboye of the Redeemed Christian Church of God, Dr. David Oyedepo of the Living Faith Church, and Dr. Myres Muroe of the Bahamas Faith in Bahamas.

INTRODUCTION

This book has taken me a huge amount of time, meditation, reasoning, effort, research, consultation, observation and studies to write. The title was first published as an eight- page article. After the publication, the response was very impressive. I began to receive numerous calls from people commending me on the article. Most of them asserted the fact that the article had changed their lives. That is why I have now decided to make it in a more elaborate form by putting it in form of a book. I know that by doing so, it would get across to hundreds, thousands and millions of ladies.

Today, one of the leading problems facing our communities, societies, nations and even the World at large is that most mature ladies are finding it extremely difficult to get married. The statistics of those ladies from one country to another is enormous and increasing at a faster rate. To be estimate, out of the over two billion ladies in the World today, over 70% who are mature enough are desperately looking for marriage partners.. This book is written to help those mature ladies get married and also to reveal to the upcoming young ladies those qualities that would make them attractive to great guys in order to avoid the mistakes millions of other ladies had made in the past. I am worried and bothered whenever I see mature ladies finding it very difficult to get married.

I have met countless number of them and a brief observation of those ladies showed why they are not getting attracted to the guys. My intense desire to help enough ladies get married to their desired partners has made me to do a lot of studies, research, meditation, reasoning and consultation to come up with the effective and proven principles of getting married, revealed in this book.

I have a dream. I have a global vision. I intend to help one billion ladies to get married to their desired spouses all over the world. I mention "desired spouse" because it does no good to get married out of frustration to a guy you don't love or one that doesn't meet your standard. Getting married to a guy you don't love passionately will only lead to a struggling, hateful, frustrated and mediocre marriage and will never make you a happier nor a fulfilled lady.

By buying this book, you potentially become one of the one billion ladies I intend to help get married to their desired guys. You only become one of those ladies if you read, note, and apply the principles in this book, get married to your desired guy and enjoy a memorable, lasting and fulfilled marriage.

I didn't write this book because of the financial gain. I would be more excited and fulfilled to hear from you or read your letters that the principles in this book have enable you to attract, court and eventually marry excellent guys that suite your values, meet your standard and make you a better, effective, powerful and fulfilled lady.
This book contains the most powerful and effective principles, secrets, tools, and strategies in history that will make you become one of the most sought-after

ladies that highly resourceful and excellent guys are eager and crave to marry. But, it can only be powerful when you inculcate and apply what you read inside this book. Knowledge is only powerful when it is put into use. A recent study showed that over 90% of the people that buy a new book never read more than the first chapter and only 20% of those that read the complete chapters apply what they have learnt in their lives. By reading and applying the principles in the context of this book; you will become a powerful, smart, effective and excellent lady that other excellent guys are willing to go the extra- mile and put the extra-effort to persuade and convince to be their wife. As Winston Churchill, one of the most excellent Prime-Minister that Great Britain has ever had, once said, *"My most brilliant achievement was my ability to be able to persuade my wife to marry me"*.

The principles and fact you are about to explore in this book will enable you to learn, cultivate and exhibit the great and remarkable qualities that will make you attract great guys to your life. You will then begin to have choice problem. Great and highly resourceful guys will be proposing marriage to you and you will then be left with making an excellent choice among these excellent guys. Over the years, I have discovered that most ladies, when they see their mates, colleagues or friends getting married, would say;

"This lady is very lucky and fortunate" They believe that marriage is a function of luck. But, I have always tried to ascertain the fact that those ladies are not fortunate; they only possess the winning qualities and treasure that make them marry the guys of their choice.

This book is a powerful revelation. It shows what you

have been doing that have been hindering you from getting married and the qualities you will have to learn and exhibit so as to attract and eventually marry excellent guys that will make you complete, unique, powerful, exciting., and fulfilled.

Festus A Toks.

1

BE A LADY OF GREAT CHARACTER.

My mother was troubled by my lack of beauty; she tried hard to bring me up well so that my manners would compensate for my looks.

----------------------------- Eleanor Roosevelt.

Former first Lady of the United States and one of the most effective women in history

THE POWER OF ATTITUDE.

Marriage is becoming very competitive. As a lady, one of your greatest dreams should be getting married to your desired partner. But, to some ladies, getting married has become so tough that they are frustrated, worried and have become an object of mockery. Most ladies, out of their desperate desire to get married get hooked to any guy that comes their way, even when such a person does not meet their standards, suite their values or functions perfectly as a spouse. What makes these ladies most of whom are well over-aged, attractive and with excellent careers find it very difficult to get married? Why do some ladies court and eventually get married to their choice partners, while others, despite having been in a number of relationships find it extremely difficult to get married.

After a lot of studies on this major problem that wanted to cause a bleak to the dreams and aspirations of millions of ladies, researchers have found that the problem is more of attitude than every other factors put together. Thousands of guys interviewed in every continent of the world said they would rather court and marry a lady with positive and winning attitude than that with any other qualities.

Attitude is the critical factor in your desire to get married. Attitude can make or mar any relationship. Attitude is the way you think and feel about somebody or yourself. It is the way you act, think and behave towards others.

Ladies that attract highly resourceful guys for courtship that eventually lead to a blissful marriage are simply ladies of great and excellent attitude. Gone are the days when beauty or other physical qualities alone could ensure you get married to your desired partner; Now, it is attitude that makes all the difference. As the French proverb says, *"Beauty unaccompanied with virtue is as a flower without perfume"*. Most ladies that are having difficulty in getting married are simply ladies of bad attitude.

Bad attitude can be devastating, destructive and could hinder you from getting married or achieving anything worthwhile in life. As Author Marvin Walberg once said, *"A negative attitude is as deadly to your job search or career as the most potent virus"*. John Maxwell, one of American Personal development trainers once said, *"Attitude is our best friend and our worst enemy"*. The attitude you learn, exhibit and demonstrate at all times will either attract or drive away potential spouse from your life.

> Beauty unaccompanied with virtue is like a flower without perfume.
> -------- French Proverb

Successful ladies that get married to their desired spouses are not more intelligent, pretty, resourceful, attractive, wealthy, or better-off than you are; they simply learn, exhibit and demonstrate some winning attitude and life enhancing manners that make them a winner in all their relationships and eventually get married to their desire spouses.

You need to have the right attitude towards friends, colleagues, family, associates and people in general. An attitude of acceptance, courtesy, kindness, respect, forgiveness, consideration and open-minded nature can play a great role in your desire to get married.

Attitude is everything. You must be a person of great attitude to marry your desired guy. Great attitude will make you a winner in all your dealing. You must learn to always demonstrate warm, positive, pleasant and open attitude to people at all times in all situations; knowing well that your attitude more than any thing else plays a vital role in your desire to get married. Attitude plays a key role in every aspect of your life. It is the single determiner of your success in family, business, relationship and professional life. As Winston Churchill, the former British Prime Minister, once said, *"Attitude is a little thing that makes a big difference"*. Highly successful relationship of any kind strived on attitude. Most courtship that would have ended in marriage have been deterred, destroyed or brought to an early end as a result of wrong attitude. Your attitude will either make you the kind of lady that guys are desperate to marry or the lady that no guy wants to get along with or marry even if you are the only unmarried lady on earth. As John Maxwell said, *"Attitude is a thing which draws people to us or repels them"*. Attitude affects every aspect of your life. It can make you a peak performer or mediocre person in your field.

It can make you a fulfilled or unfulfilled person in your marriage. It can make you a very successful business person or that without any track records. Attitude can make you a leader others are willing to follow or the one that has no influence among the followers.

> Attitude is a thing which draws people to us or repels them.
> ---------------- John Maxwell

13

ATTITUDE IS ATTRACTIVE

Right, positive and pleasant attitude make you attractive to guys. It makes you the kind of lady that great and highly resourceful guys would want to have as a friend and as you know; marriage springs from courtship and courtship springs from friendship. So, attitude is the chief initiator of the steps to marriage. Attitude reveals both your inner and outer qualities and that makes you attractive to guys and people in general. It shows what you are made up of. It reveals to others your real person. As a lady, pleasant attitude makes you attractive to guys. It makes you a lady that others want to get along with. Guys will sense a great treasure in you and be wooing you for a committed relationship that may eventually lead to a fulfilling marriage. Most ladies make the mistake of paying close attention to their outer qualities with little or no attention to their inner qualities.

They want to look attractive outside, but not inside and that is the reason they are not getting attracted to guys. Highly successful ladies that get married to their desired guys are those that are very attractive both inside and outside. They possess both the inner and outer qualities that enhance their desire to get married. Pleasant attitude is the inner quality that makes you attractive to the person of the opposite sex and people in general.

BE A LADY OF GREAT CHARACTER

Character is the feature and quality that differentiate one person from another. It is a strong personal quality such as the ability to deal with difficult or dangerous situations. No guys want to marry any lady with flaw character. That's why a close attention must be paid to how you treat, act or respond to people or situations at all times. Most ladies are of the opinion that because they are pretty, beautiful or have some attractive physical qualities; it would be very easy for them to get married and never pay close attention to their character. I have no doubt that your physical qualities may get you into courtship; but it will take a pleasant and strong character to keep, protect, sustain and ensure that the relationship leads to the desired end; Marriage. As the Nigerian proverb says, *"Your character is your beauty"*. Strong and positive character makes all the difference in your desire to get married.

> Your character is your beauty.
> -------- Nigerian Proverb

There are millions of pretty and very attractive ladies out there finding it very difficult to get hooked to the guy of their choice as a marriage partner due to their flaw and unpleasant character, whereas some other ladies who are not so attractive outwardly, but possess some deep, strong and unquestionable character are getting attracted and married to their desired guys. Character is the foundation for any successful courtship that will eventually lead to successful marriage. There is no substitute for deep, positive and pleasant character for any lady that desire to get married to a highly resourceful guy. As a wise man once said, *"Youth and beauty fade, but character endures forever"*. You cannot be more successful in any relationship than the state of your character. No lady can climb beyond the limitation of her character. A deep and pleasant character makes you to cope with all the up's and down's in your relationship and life's experiences. It makes you a lady that guys are willing to marry. Your character speak louder than what you say. You must begin to treat everyone irrespective of status and condition with recognition, respect and polite behavior. You must be people's person and demonstrate unquestionable character to people at all times in every situations. *People pay close attention to what you do than what you say.*

> Youth and beauty fade, but character Endures forever.
> ------ Wise Saying

Having a good, deep, strong, and pleasant character can enable you to become one of the most sought after ladies guys want to have as a spouse. I recently watched a television show titled, "couple's time" where one of the most influential and popular Nigerian actress; Omotola Jalade was the guest with her spouse. The interviewer asked the couple, "how did you both meet" and the husband who said he had just arrived from abroad when they met, said his elder sister had been observing Omotola over the time in their local church, discovered she possessed some great character and introduced the couple to each other. There is no doubting the fact that Omotola is a very pretty lady coupled with a lucrative career, but her deep, unquestionable and pleasant character played a vital role in her getting married to her desired spouse. Perhaps, there are other prettier ladies than Omotola in the movie industry today finding it very difficult to get married as a result of their flaw and unwelcome character.

Pleasant character is a learned attitude. You can make a committed effort today to cultivate a winning character and replace all those flaws-manners of yours with good-manners. Pastor Billy Graham said,

"When wealth is lost, nothing is lost, but when character is lost, all is lost". Character is the foundation of every successful personal, business, career and marriage relationship.

As the African proverb says, *"Character is the commander of fortune"*.

Deep, pleasant and strong character is one the greatest qualities you can ever possess to attract great guys for marriage. That's why there are millions of highly attractive ladies out there still finding it difficult to get married as a result of their flaw character. I recently met a lady and told my colleague; "This lady is going to become hot cake for guys to marry". She has a very strong, positive, pleasant and unquestionable character that you can hardly find in the 21st century ladies. She treats everyone politely, respectively and above all, she appreciates everyone that comes her way. I am not surprised she got married to her desired guy just few months after I met her. You too can cultivate this winning character and become the lady guys are eager to have as their life partner. The kind that would make highly resourceful guys to be desperate to have you as their spouse and want to stay with you for all the days of their life.

> Character is the commander of fortune.
> ------ African proverb

It takes a good character to initiate, keep, and sustain any courtship that will lead to a successful marriage. Pleasant character makes you to become a celebrity and until you become one; you cannot marry a celebrity. Deep character makes you endure every situation and circumstance without wavering towards the future.

Deep and strong character enables you to develop tolerance and growth, overcome obstacles, face challenges of life and handle success effectively.

> * Are you irritable?
> * Are you impatient?
> * Are you difficult to get along with?
> * Are you rude and thoughtless?

All these are flaw character that will drive away guys from you.

STRATEGIES FOR MOULDING A WINNING CHARACTER;

It takes a conscious decision

The starting point of moulding a winning character that will make you a winner in all your relationships is to take a conscious decision and resolute determination to replace those flaw character that has been hindering you from getting married with some winning character that will make you a better person and the kind of lady that guys want to get along with. You must accept the fact that you possess some unwelcome, unpleasant and flaw manners and character that requires your constant and personal resolution to be replaced with a deep, strong and pleasant character. You must take absolute responsibility for your character and take an intense desire to learn, cultivate, exhibit and demonstrate the winning and quality character that will make guys chase you as "Bees chase honey" for marriage.

Thousands and millions of ladies who have been unable to marry due to their flaw and nasty manners before have suddenly taken a resolute decision at a point in their lives to learn, cultivate and exhibit good manners and character that make them attracted to great and highly resourceful guys and eventually get married to the men of their choice. By the law of emulation; what others have done before, you can do the same now and get the same or even better results.

> You are the architect of your character.
> ---------- Festus Toks

Accept it or not, you are responsible for your character. You are the architect of your character. Your character is the sum of all your beliefs, experiences you have had, the decision you have taken, those you refused to take in the past, and the attitude you have learned as you grew up from your parents, guardians, friends, colleagues and mates. The good thing is that anything learned can as well be unlearned through personal decision, dedication and commitment. That is why you must accept absolute responsibility for your character and be willing to replace those flaw characters of yours with some pleasant behaviors that will make you a winner in all your relationships and enable you to marry your desired guy.

Emerson said, *"The basis of good manners is self-reliance"*.

Can you rely on your character? You must accept total responsibility for your character and take a personal decision, determination and commitment to learn those manners that will make others want to do things with you, for you or get along with you; be it in relationship, business, or any endeavour of life. Highly successful and resourceful ladies that get attracted to and married the guys of their choice are simply ladies of great character. They accept total responsibility for their character and take a conscious decision to learn the winning manners that makes them a winner in all their relationships. Some of them have had it very tough in the past, influenced by parents' bad manners, experienced some bad incidents, get disappointed by many guys, had many courtship failures and passed through many challenges as a result of their character. But, at a point in their lives, they accept total responsibility for their flaw character, take absolute control of their future and bring out time to learn deep, strong and unquestionable character that enable them to get married to their desired guys and become fulfilled in life. The World-renowned entertainer, Oprah Winfrey was raped as a child by her cousin. But, she never allowed this and many other bad experiences she had early in life stop her from moulding a winning character that enabled her to reach the peak of success in her personal, relationship, career, and community life. Writer John Didron said,

"Character; the willingness to accept responsibility for ones own life ------ is the source from which self-respect springs" Deep, strong and unquestionable character enable guys want to deal with and get along with you. It makes you look responsible, respected and desirable to people. That is why you must take a conscious decision

and resolute determination today to mould a winning character for yourself. You must accept the fact that your flaw character has been hindering, preventing and causing great havoc to every of your effort to get married and be willing to make a change. Change is the price of progress. Until you decide to change; nothing will be changed in your life. If you keep doing the same things; you will keep getting the same results. That is why you must take a conscious decision to change from those flaw acts of yours and begin to learn and demonstrate unquestionable character towards people at all times in every circumstance. it does not matter what has happened to you in the past; what does matter is that you begin to eliminate those flaw character of yours and begin to learn the winning character that will makes you the lady that guys are desperate, anxious and eager to take to the altar for marriage.

> The unexamined life is not
> worth living.
> ------- Socrates

CHARACTER IS A LEARNABLE ATTITUDE

Deep, pleasant and winning character is not inborn, inherited, inherent or ready made; it's a learnt attitude.
As Psychologist Edna Lyall Said, "Character is not ready made; it is created bit by bit". I have seen ladies who get it very tough to get married due to their flaw characters, but suddenly take a decision to change their flaw manners. They decide to eliminate every of their flaw acts in order to learn, exhibit and demonstrate pleasant character and eventually get married to their desire guys and enjoy a fulfilled marriage. Perhaps, you have had it very difficult getting married in the past; you can begin today to learn the winning character that will attract positive, pleasant and potential spouse to your life. It doesn't take much effort, difficulty or stress to eliminate those flaw manners that have held you back for many years and replace them now with deep, pleasant and unquestionable acts that will make you attractive to guys. But, it does take personal decision, commitment

and determination to learn, cultivate and demonstrate those acts that will make you a lady that guys are eager to marry. *Repetition is the key to perfection.* What you do repeatedly eventually becomes an integral part of your life.

Psychiatrists said it takes the average person about 30 repetitions of an activity to turn it into a habit. Begin right now to face and eliminate your flaw character and replace them with deep, strong and pleasant character. Take a bold and continuous step to work on yourself till you become the lady that guys want to initiate any meaningful relationships with.

You must always be polite, pleasant and just in all your dealings with people. Chances make our parents, races, color and background but choices make our character. As Author Mary Wortley Montagu said, *"Politeness costs nothing and gains everything"*. It takes a staunch commitment to learn any attitude that will make you a better and fulfilled lady. You must be dedicated and committed to learning and demonstrating deep and great character in all you do, say and think.

> Politeness costs nothing and gains everything.
> ------------ Mary Wortley Montagu

TAKE AN HONEST INVENTORY OF YOURSELF.

To mould a winning and attractive character for yourself, you must be disciplined enough to take an honest self-inventory and also correct every deficiency. You know your various faults and shortcomings better than anyone else. You have the better knowledge of yourself. It's amazing why most ladies are never truthful to themselves. They are trying to po rtray to the public what they are not inside. *Self-deception is the greatest and most destructive deception on earth.* That's why you cannot afford to deceive yourself.

> Self-deception is the greatest and most destructive deception on earth.
> ------------------ Festus Toks

As a lady that desires to mould a winning character that will make you a winner in any relationship; you must apply the rule of "self-analysis". This rule says, "You begin to analyze every of your acts, behaviours and manners to know which of them that has been driving away or drawing people to your life". You must begin to examine yourself to know those acts that have hindered you from getting married over the years. You must be sincere with yourself in doing this. You are the master of your life. Nobody knows you more than you do. No one can say more about you than your real self. Even, there are limits to what your parents, relations, cousins, friends or mates can say about you. If you will be sincere with yourself; you know those acts that easily turn off people from you. You know people's complaint about your attitude. You know what you have done in the past that have not spoken well of you. You know those acts responsible for the failure of your past relationships. The starting point of moulding a winning character is to do intensive analysis of all your ill-manners and take a conscious decision to replace them with pleasant and positive ones. Self- examination helps to know your self-fault and thereby replace your faulty manners with quality character. To be ignorant of your flaw manners can take you backward in the journey of marriage for years and may hinder you from achieving your marriage goals. As Socrates once said, "The unexamined life is not worth living". That's why you must always examine yourself in all area of your life.

That's one of the greatest qualities of every effective, competent and fulfilled lady that enjoys excellent marriage. They are always examining themselves to know their shortcomings. If you will be sincere to yourself; you know what makes guys to easily get tired of you.

* How do you react to people irrespective of status, position or personality of that person?

* How do you handle difficult circumstances, situations and experiences?

* How do you react when someone wrongs you or doesn't meet up to your expectations?

* How do you react to guys when they cannot fulfill their promises to you due to one reason or the other?

* How do you handle new achievement, success or breakthrough you experience in your life?

* Are you rude, thoughtless or thoughtful?

* Are you easily angered?

* Are you impatient?

* Are you arrogant and proud?
* Are you very difficult to understand and get

along with?

* Are you understandable and respectable?

* Are you dependable and reliable?

* Are you very positive despite negative experiences of life?

All these and many more are the cues to your character. You must be very sincere to yourself. You know what you did when people praised or rebuked you. As a lady aspiring to get married, probably, you've have had two or more relationship in the past that never lead to your desired end. If you will be sincere with yourself, you know what you did that made those guys not continue with the relationships. If you will sincerely reflect on your attitude, manners and behaviours; you know those that have made people to celebrate or ridicule you. It does no good trying to deceive yourself. You know quite well that you are responsible for most of the broken and unproductive relationships experienced in the past. You know what you did that made those guys quit the relationship even months to tying up the marital knot. You cannot be doing the same things and expect to get different results.

It is worrisome that most ladies keep doing the same thing that makes every of their relationship end in a crash and never take-out time to work on themselves. They keep blaming other people, circumstances, their spouses, parents and friends for their misfortune whereas they are the chief cause of their problems. If this is the way you think; you need to understand that you are the chief cause of your misfortune and be willing to work on yourself to become the lady that guys are eager to marry. You are responsible for your broken relationship and nobody is coming to the rescue. As the timeless saying goes, "If it is to be, it is up to me".

> Ultimately, people shape their own character.
> ----------- Anne Frank

You must accept total responsibility for your life and begin right now to eliminate every of your bad and unwelcome character that have deterred you from getting married. Self-examination springs to self-adjustment that leads to self-fulfillment. You must examine yourself to discover your flaw character and begin to adjust your character to the one that will make you a happier, more prosperous and fulfilled lady.

PAY CLOSE ATTENTION TO EVERY OF YOUR ACTS.

To mould a winning character for yourself, you must pay close attention and accept responsibility for every of your acts. Each of your actions in an indication of your belief. That's why you must have a positive belief-system. You must be very sensitive of how you treat people, react to situations and be master of your emotions. Baltasar Said, *"Reputation depends mostly on what is hidden than on what is seen"*. You must be very consistent in your actions and be a lady of your words. You must cultivate winning qualities in the inside by letting positive thinking and words dominate your thoughts. You must make a commitment to always demonstrate respect to authority, personal integrity in all you do and say, wholesome thoughts and says pure words at all times in every circumstance.

There is an African Proverb that says, "Character is who you are when nobody is watching". You cannot fake good character on the outside when you don't have it in the inside. You cannot pretend to make-up or be a lady of pleasant, deep or unquestionable character. It must spring and originate from your inside. That's why you must take a conscious decision to let positive things dominate your thoughts. Have positive outlooks towards life.

You cannot pretend to your spouses that you are a lady of pleasant character when you are not. Trying to do this will not help your relationship or make you accomplish your marriage goals. Time will definitely reveal your real self to the opposite sex and this may hinder your ability to get married. That's why you must consciously learn and cultivate the inner qualities that will make you a success in all your relationships.

> Character is who you are when
> nobody is watching.
> --------- African Proverb

You must pay close attention to every of your acts not pretending to be a lady of pleasant manners when you are not. You must decide to live uprightly, justly, modestly and faithfully in all your actions to people at all times in every circumstance. You must always be yourself and never panic to say, think, feel and express what is right and just in your entire life endeavour. A wise man once said, *"Character is made by many acts and destroyed by one act"*

You must always exhibit unquestionable character to

people at all times. You must always pay close attention to every of your act knowing fully well that your acts end up to making your character.

> Character is made by many acts
> and destroyed by one act.
> ----------- Wise saying

BE POSITIVE TO DIFFICULT SITUATIONS

One of the ways to becoming a lady of winning and unquestionable character is to always have positive attitude, approach and response to every difficulty and challenges you may experience in life. The ability to handle difficult situations positively has a long deal to say about your character. You must always have it in mind that every bad experience, situation or up's and down's you may experience at any point in life is for a moment and will make you learn and grow if you are able to face them with positive attitude. Adversity, challenges and difficulties are among the true test of a person's character. How do you respond to people when things are not going on has been expected? With positive attitude, the bad experiences of life groom you to become a better lady. As Seneca said, *"Adversity strengthens the body"* It takes a deep character to develop tolerant, growth, face and overcome bad experiences of life. That's why you must have positive attitude towards the up's and down's and experiences of your life; knowing fully well that every experience of life has telling statement on the contents of your character.

A person's character is that person's security in any endeavour of life. If you constantly stand for justice or what is right in every of your dealings, you won't regret your action or inaction in any circumstances of your life. Most ladies compromise their character when going through harsh challenges of life. But, as a success-minded lady that desire excellence in every aspect of your life; you must develop the inner qualities that will enable you endure every tough challenges you may experience without having a question mark in your character.

> Adversity strengthens the body.
> -------- Seneca

Having positive and right attitudes towards every life's challenges enable you to develop tolerance and perseverance that will make you pass the test of character and integrity and become a very competent, effective and admirable lady. If you always focus on how things can begin to work rather than why things are not working; you will develop inner qualities that will enable you overcome and pass the test of life. Some ladies are too problem-oriented that they never think of what to do to fix what is not working in their lives. These ladies always resolve to cutting corners to mend things, therefore putting their character to a state of questioning.

The success-minded ladies are solution-oriented.
They are always concerned about what to do to avoid further relationship break-up rather than blaming other people or circumstances for all their broken relationships. They are always thinking of the right things to do to have a working relationship and thereby better their lives without putting their character in a state of coma or questioning. To become the lady of deep, trusted and unquestionable character; you must possess inner qualities and strength that will make you have a

positive approach and attitude towards every situations and up's and down's in your life. You must never cut corners when facing and handling the challenges of life. You must handle every bad experience positively and with tolerant attitudes. That is the only way you will cultivate the admirable character that will make you become the lady that great guys are eager to marry.

KEEP WORKING ON YOURSELF.

To become a more successful, happier and more fulfilled lady, you must keep working on your character. You must continue to learn, cultivate and exhibit great qualities that will attract great guys to your life. As Pat Riley, the foremost NBA coach once said, "When you stop striving to get better; you're bound to get worse". You must never be satisfied with the state of your character. You must continue to work on your character and demonstrate great qualities to people at all times in every situation. You must be very conscious of every of your act; knowing fully well that a single unwelcome and nasty act can tarnish the reputation you've built over the years.

To really become a lady of great character; you must have daily assessment of your acts. You must continue to examine every of your act and habit and always think of how to make them better.

As a lady that desires to attract great guys for marriage; you must continue to improve your character. You must always be mindful and cautious of every of your act and make an unrelenting efforts to always turn out appropriate acts, deeds and attitudes that suite the situations.

A lady's reputation is the sum of her character and reputation is built over a period of time. But, the most frustrating thing is that reputation which is built by many acts and can be destroyed by one act and a wounded reputation is seldom repaired. That's why you must be very mindful of every of your act; turning out unquestionable character to build a great reputation for yourself.

> When you stop striving to get better;
> you are bound to get worse.
> ---------- Pat Riley

Perhaps, one of the greatest things you can ever do to build great reputation is to keep working on yourself. You must take a staunch decision to keep improving your act, behaviour and attitude to become a more pleasant, friendly and character-wise lady. You must never be satisfied with the state of your character. You must always desire to turn-out something better and become a more organized and happier lady. You must always learn, cultivate and exhibit the inner qualities and strength that will make you a master of every circumstances and situations.

You must always make committed effort to work, build and refine your character to become the lady that highly organized guys are willing to get along with and desire as a spouse.

A person is the architect of his own character. You must make a resolute decision to keep working on yourself and build the winning character that will make you a winner in all relationship. You must take a deliberate step to work on yourself and continue turning out great acts that will make you a lady that highly responsible guys are desperate, eager, and willing to marry.

> Perfection is attained by slow progress.
> It requires the hand of time.
> -------- Voltaire

To become a lady of unquestionable character, you must always take a daily examination of every of your act and be humble enough to fix every of your wrong acts and always walk on yourself to become a better person. Perfection doesn't happen overnight, it takes a deliberate decision to work on yourself over a period of time. As Writer Voltaire said, *"Perfection is attained by slow progress; it requires the hand of time"*. That's why you must make a continuous effort to always work on yourself. You must always think of how to improve your character that will make you a perfect and more organized lady and thereby attract potential spouse to your life.

CHARACTER IS POWER

Character is your stronghold in every of your relationship and life's dealing.

The content of your character determines the state, pace and height of your success in any relationship. Character can be a stepping stone or stumbling block in your desire to get married. Deep and unquestionable character makes you a master of every life's situation. It makes you face and overcome life's challenges without cutting corners or compromising your integrity. Deep and unquestionable character makes you a lady that highly responsible guys are running after for marriage. *Great character is what adds colour to your beauty*. Deep and pleasant character makes you a winner in all your relationships. Deep, quality, pleasant and unquestionable character makes you a lady of power and influence among people.

> Great character is what adds colour to your beauty.
> ——— Festus Toks

Great character makes you a lady of influence among people and when guys see that you command great attention among people; they will want to get along with you. Pleasant and quality character makes you a more fulfilled lady. It makes you attractive to guys and people in general. There is no doubting the fact that your character is one of the greatest qualities that determine your ability to get married. A recent study of over 500 lasting, successful and fulfilled marriages show that; these highly fulfilled ladies possessed unquestionable and winning character that attracts them to their various spouses.

Character is the initiator and sustainer of any relationship. It takes a quality character to make any marriage a lasting and memorable experience. That's why there are countless number of marriage break-ups in our World today. A recent study showed that over 60% of new marriages in America always end up in divorce within two years of the relationship and that's how it is in all nations of the World. These couples just lack the winning character to keep and sustain their relationships.

As a lady, your character is the greatest quality in your desire to get married. Highly responsible guys can compromise other qualities; but the quality of pleasant character. Character is the bedrock of any lasting relationship and marriage. That's why you must learn and cultivate the winning character that will make you a winner in all your relationships.

Remember, a lady of character is a lady of power. A lady of power is a lady of influence. A lady of influence is a master of relationship and when you are a master of relationship; you attract all the great, responsible guys and potential spouse to your life and become a happier and more fulfilled lady.

BE A LADY OF GREAT CHARACTER

1. Your character is a critical factor in your desire to get married. Flaw character constitutes an insurmountable obstacle to any attempt to attract great guys for marriage.

2. Great character is a magnet of great and highly responsible guys for marriage. You must cultivate the right, positive and pleasant attitudes that will make you attractive to guys.

3. The starting point of moulding a winning character is to take an honest inventory of yourself and correct every deficiency in your manners. You must accept responsibility for your faulty characters and be willing to make a change.

4. Great character is what adds color to your beauty. Make a resolute determination to develop the inner qualities that will make you attractive on the outside.

5. Your characters are learned and can be unlearned. Resolve today to unlearn every flaw manners that has held you back from getting married over the years. You must be sincere with yourself in doing this.

6. Highly resourceful guys can substitute quality character to average physical qualities. Resolve today to cultivate the quality character that will make you attract quality guys for marriage.

2

BE A LADY OF GREAT DREAMS TOWARDS THE FUTURE.

The most pathetic person in the World is someone who has sight but has no vision.

-----------Helen Keller.

The first women Harvard University ever recognized with an honorary degree.

To become the lady that highly resourceful guys are eager to marry; you must have well articulated dreams and aspirations towards the future. Marriage is a lifetime journey; and no purposeful, resourceful and success-minded guy will want to get along with any lady that has no dreams or plans towards the future. Those ladies that live their lives on chances without any meaningful aspirations towards the future hardly command the attention of great guys for marriage. That's why ladies that are very ambitious about the future; desire great things in life and walking towards accomplishing their aims always end up attracting highly resourceful and ambitious guys for marriage.

Because like attracts like, Ladies that desire great things in life always end up marrying great guys. Likewise, those with low aims end up marrying guys that have low aims toward the future; and those ladies that have no plans at all end up marrying guys that have no destination point in life. But, various studies have attested to the fact that highly ambitious ladies are the most sought-after ladies for marriage.

Recently, I met a lady that was very anxious to get married. She is very pretty but has no dreams or expectations towards the future. She has no master plan for her life. Perhaps, this is the reason she never get any guy to woo her for marriage despite her attractive physical qualities. All she was concerned about was getting married. Nothing more; nothing else. She has no career plans. That's how most ladies live their lives. They have no major plans for their lives. They just want to get married and believe the guy should be responsible for everything. But highly ambitious guys can easily be turned-off by ladies that have no plans towards the future. That's why average ladies with well-articulated goals towards the future will definitely command the attention of highly resourceful and ambitious guys for marriage. That's why you must have cut-plan and great goals towards your future. Sense of goals makes you an asset to guys.

Most ambitious guys will do everything possible to avoid having a liability as a spouse. When guys can sense that you have well articulated plans and take every step to reach your goals; they will take it as a privilege having you as their spouse, knowing fully well that the relationship will hasten their journey to the top.

> Most ambitious guys will rather remain single than have a liability as a spouse.
> -------------- Festus Toks

HAVE A MASTER PLANS FOR YOUR LIFE.

As a lady aspiring to marry your choice partner; you must have a well-articulated master plan for your life. You must have goals you desire to accomplish at every stage of your life. You must know where you are going in life; know where you are and what it takes to reach your life's destination.

If you are not a purposeful lady; you cannot attract purposeful guys to your life. That's why you must develop a clear-cut goals you desire to achieve in every aspect of your life. No ambitious guy will want to marry any lady without dreams, goals and great aspirations towards the future. As a matter of fact, nothing can be more frustrating, devastating or lead to unsuccessful and mediocre life than living without dreams, goals or future aspirations. As a wise man once said, "*A person without a dream is a disaster going somewhere to happen*". Helen Keller, the woman who became blind, deaf and dumb at the childhood age of 11 months old, but eventually accomplished remarkable success in her life and even had her name in the Guinness World book of record once maintained; *"The most pathetic person in the World is not the one without sight, but the one without dream"*. What you dream determines what you will eventually become.

> Highly fulfilled ladies are goal-driven.
> -------- Festus Toks

One of the fundamental qualities of highly fulfilled ladies is that they are goal-oriented. Success of any kind is never achieved by mistake or luck; it results from a goal driven life. As David Schwartz maintained, *"Goals are essential to success as air to life"*. That's why you must have well-articulated goals toward the future. No guy desires to marry any lady that doesn't know where she's going to in life. You must have great goals towards your future and be optimistic in pursuing your goals despite mistakes, challenges, failures or obstacles knowing fully well that successful ladies overcome seemingly insurmountable obstacles to achieve their life's dreams.

Most ladies have a very wrong orientation towards marriage. They believe their man should be responsible for all the family responsibilities and affairs; and as a result, never set goals for themselves or desire to be productive and contribute to the family. These ladies always find it very difficult to get married. Most guys want to marry an asset and not a liability. That's why you must be extremely goal-oriented and be productive in life.

You must desire great goals to be accomplished at every stage of your life.

You must have great agitation and aspiration towards the future. You must desire a masterpiece for your life. When you have great goals towards the future; you will eventually attract and marry great guys. When guys can see you're going somewhere in life; that you are future-oriented; have great future aspirations and goals; and taking every step to reach your desired end; they will be interested to have you as their spouse. They can see you going towards a glorious future and be willing to go along with you; knowing fully well that both of you will be better-off as spouse.

STRATEGIES FOR GOAL SETTING.

A success-minded lady must have goals to be accomplished in every aspect of her life. To really become a very fulfilled lady that will attract highly resourceful guys for marriage; you must desire great things to be accomplished in your;

*   Career life

*   Relationship life

*   Financial life

*   Marital life

*   Spiritual life

*   Community life

As a lady who desires to marry great guys and achieve great things in life; you must be goal-oriented in all aspect of your life.

You must have a well articulated master-plan to be achieved at every stage of your life.

CAREER GOALS.

Only two out of every ten ladies have career goals. Most of the 21st century ladies are too obsessed with getting married that they have no viable and meaningful career goals for their lives. They believe the man should be responsible for all the home responsibilities. If you really want to become the lady that highly resourceful guys are eager to marry; you must set goals you want to accomplish in your field, profession or career. You must decide the position you want to attain in your organization; know what it takes to get there and be willing to fully pay the prize of making your dreams become a reality.

Are you self-employed, work with the Government or private organization? You must decide what you want to accomplish in your profession in the weeks, months and years ahead that will make you a more competent, happier, more successful and more fulfilled lady. We live in a world that changes at a faster pace. That's why you must keep setting goals for your life. You must keep upgrading your skills, records and achievement, because the success of today may not give you all the satisfaction and fulfillment in the nearer future. You must desire to reach the peak in your Organization, desire what it takes to get there and make unrelenting efforts to reach your desired end.

One of the ways to remain relevant in your field and life as a whole is to keep setting goals for your life. You must never be contented with what you've accomplished in the past; you must desire to achieve greater things in the nearer future.

> No man can accomplish great things in life without the help and co-operation of others.
> -------- ------ Napoleon Hill

RELATIONSHIP GOALS.

The quality of your relationship determines the quality of your life. Relationship is very crucial to achieving your goals in life; fully utilizing your potentials or becoming a more fulfilled lady. As the 17th century philosopher, Napoleon hill said, "*No man can accomplish great things in life without the help and co-operation of others*". That's why you must set relationship goals for your life. You must constantly think of the relationship you can develop, initiate and maintain that will complement your efforts towards your desired ends.

Relationship can make or mar your future. Some relationship can hinder your desire to get married. As a lady that desires great things in life; you must eliminate every unproductive relationship and make a committed effort to keep, sustain and maintain your productive and result-oriented relationships.

Relationships are crucial to reaching your life's destination. That's why you must never be involved in any heartbreaking or dreams-shattering relationship.

As Author George Pettie once said, "*It is better to be alone than in ill company*". Wrong association has held many ladies back from getting married than any other factors you can ever consider.

I have seen some ladies that have nice character and highly resourceful, but have wrong orientation as a result of the bad influence of wrong association. Most of these ladies like having fun, dating married, rich and well-to-do guys without considering their marital life. By the time they realize that their attitudes is wrong and desire to change; it is almost very difficult to have a responsible guys taking them to the altar for marriage, because they must have really messed up their lives all these while and age will really be telling on them. That's why you must have a sense of association. You must associate with those friends that have positive attitude, image and very optimistic about the future.

> It is better to be alone than in ill company.
> -------- George Pettie

As a lady that desires to get married; it does no good to associate with ladies that have no marriage values or those that are into illicit drugs, go out with different kinds of men or are involved in crooked activities. You must have a sense of relationship and associate with those friends that will hasten your journey to your desired end.

FINANCIAL GOALS.

To become a very fulfilled lady; you must have goals concerning your financial life.

How much are you earning right now? How much is your monthly and annual income? How much do you want to earn in months and years ahead? What can you do to really increase your income in years ahead? What other training or skills can you learn that will increase your net-worth? You must have well articulated financial goals for your life. Great financial future is as a result of long term financial planning. You must have goals of how much you want to worth at every stage of your life.

To really secure a bright financial future for your life; you must have a long term financial planning and invest your money in income-generating assets. You must be extreme-investors. You must have well articulated monthly investing goals. You must have long term investment perspective. You must endeavour to invest your money long term enough to generate great returns for your future. Having an articulated financial goal enables you to secure a bright financial future. It makes you an asset to your spouse. It makes you command respect from guys because they can sense you are not a liability but a better spouse. Most people desire to get rich; but they have no long-term financial planning. The agitation of millions of people today is instant riches. They want to become wealthy overnight. But great financial fortune never comes this way; it comes through a long term well articulated financial planning. Great financial acumens have long-term perspective towards investing. You must be disciplined enough to invest your income wisely and long term enough in income-generating assets.

APPLY THE RULES OF 10%;

This is an investment strategy that has secured great financial fortune for millions of ladies all over the World. This rule says that "You invest 10% of your every income into income generating asset for a long period of time" You must pay yourself first by investing 10% of all your income to buying assets and stocks. When you cultivate the habit of investing from every money that comes your way; you are laying a solid financial foundation for your future and chances are excellent that you will end up a very wealthy lady in the future.

I once read about Oprah Winfrey who is today one of the richest people in America. Though, Oprah was born of poor parents and passed through a lot of challenges and struggles while growing up as a child. But, she learned early enough in life to invest from every dollar that comes her way. While her friends will be buying Reebok wears, pants and snickers; Oprah would decide to buy Reebok stocks. What an intelligent decision! Today, Oprah Winfrey is the highest paid entertainer in the World and one of the richest Women in history. Financial accumulation has little to do with parental foundation; it has much to do with personal resolution, commitment and financial planning.

> Association can make or mar
> your desire to get married.
> ----------- Festus Toks

As a lady who desires to secure a strong financial future; you must have a long-term financial planning. Most ladies have made themselves burden and liability to guys. They believe the man should be responsible for everything and begin to make outrageous demand on their spouses. Because they have no financial planning, no saving or genuine source of income; they begin to look up to their spouses for all their financial responsibities; and when the man cannot meet up with their financial expectations; there begins a serious misunderstanding that may eventually degenerate into breakdown of the marriage. Most marriage breakdown has its root in financial problems. A recent studies show that over 75% of problems in marriages all over the continent results from financial factors. That's why you must have a great financial planning towards the future. As the Jamaican proverb says, "Save money and money will save you". As a lady, having a well articulate financial planning towards the future makes you become an asset to your spouse. It deprives you from becoming a burden to your guy. Though, it is widely believe that the man should be responsible for all the financial responsibility of marriage. But, marriages in which both couple contributes towards the success of their home accomplish greater things faster than the ordinary one. It removes the financial burdens that have ended millions of marriages all over the World. Most relationships have been broken down due to the excessive financial demand of ladies.

But when you are a lady that doesn't inconvenience your guy with excessive financial burden; you command great respect from guys; maintain your self-worth and becomes the favorite of great guys for marriage.

> Save money and money will save you.
> ----------Jamaican Proverb

Everything is changing. Traditionally, people's values, belief and culture are all changing at a faster rate; and any person who refuses to adapt to the changing world will become obsolete. In the olden days; our tradition says that men should be totally responsible for all the financial responsibility of the relationship or marriage. The culture says that the man should totally responsible for all the financial demand at home. This belief has made most ladies to become a liability to their guys. But, today all this belief are changing at a faster rate. Most guys now prefer ladies whom they can plan their lives together with. They want ladies that have something to contribute to the success of the home. As the timeless saying goes, *"Two are better than one"*. If you really desire to get married faster; you must not be held by this belief. You must have a financial planning for your life and marriage. This attitude will make you an asset to your guy.

> Two are better than one.
> ----- Timeless sayings

Having a long term financial planning and direction makes you a favourite of highly resourceful guys for marriage. That's why you must set financial goals for yourself and make a continuous effort to reach all your goals.

MARRIAGE GOALS

It is worrisome that most ladies who desire to get married have no clear-cut marital goals for themselves. They just desire to get married but never take out time to identify, or form the mental image of;

* The kind of man they desire as a spouse.

* The qualities desired in the guy.

* The values of the guy.

* The physical qualities of the Guy

* The religious values of the guy

Most ladies desire to get married but never take out time to clarify the kind of man they desire as a spouse and thereby get married to any guy that comes there way; even when such a guy doesn't possess the qualities they desired. As Michael De Moritaigne said, *"No wind favors him who has no destined port"*. The foremost Philosopher, Seneca said, *"If a person knows not what harbor he seeks; any wind is the right wind"*. As a lady that desires to get married; it is extremely important you set a standard for the kind of guy you desire to marry. You must not marry anyhow. You must have a good understanding of what you desire in the guy with whom you want to spend the rest of your life.

Having a clear goal and understanding of the man you want prevents you from courting any guy who is not a potential marriage partner thereby avoid any emotional entangles that may result from any unproductive relationship. Having marriage goals enable you to court and eventually marry the guy that suite your values and meet your standard. It enables you to carry on a successful courtship that will lead to a successful and fulfilled marriage.

> If a person knows not what harbor he seeks; any wind is the right wind.
> ---------- Seneca

The choice of a marriage partner must be personal and should not be influenced by any external factors. This is one of the greatest choices you will ever make in your life and that is why you cannot afford to make the choice anyhow. You must make the marriage-choice based on the man that meets your personal values and standard. Having a clear-cut marriage goals enable you to have a clear understanding of what you desire in a man and ensure that you court and eventually marry the guy that meet your standard, suite your values and make you a fulfilled lady.

SPIRITUAL GOALS

As a lady who desires to get married; it is extremely important you make every effort and attempt to enhance your spiritual insight. You must make every of your decision based on God's principles. Ignorance is probably the greatest enemy of men.

As Shakespeare said, *"There is no darkness; but ignorance"*.Having a deep understanding of God's principles and strategies puts you in control of every of your life's situations. It makes you to understand the vital and fundamental principles of excellent marriage. That's why you must make unrelenting efforts to keep improving and enhancing your knowledge of God's principles. The quality of your relationship with God determines the height of your success in all endeavour of life. So, you must let God be your ultimate in life. You must maintain a workable relationship with God.

> There is no darkness; but ignorance.
> ------------ Shakespeare

There are two kinds of discovery that have no substitute in achieving outstanding and noteworthy success in life. The discovery of God and self-discovery are vital requirement to reaching the top in all endeavours of human field. God-discovery enables you to understand the fundamental principles that make the marriage relationship a fulfilled and long lasting experience. It enables you to understand God's principles and ideas in dealing with every aspect of life's situations. While self-discovery enables you to know the talents, potentials and abilities that God has endowed you with that will make you relevant in life. The discovery of self is the discovery of life. Having a workable relationship with God enables you to discover yourself and thereby achieve greater things in life. Living according to God's principles enables you to cultivate the winning attitude that will make you a winner in all relationships. It makes men run after you for marriage; because they can sense your faith values. I strongly believe that your relationship with God makes all the difference in your desire to get married. When you do your best; God will always do the rest.

> The discovery of self is the discovery of life.
> ------- Festus Toks

In a study conducted recently in the United States concerning the marriage institution; the researchers found that "spirituality and effective communication" are the two most important factors that determine the success of any marriage relationship. Couples that have great faith and living according to God's principles are able to tolerate and endure all up's and down's in their relationship. If you are a lady that want to get married to your desired guy; then, you must be a person of great faith in God. This attitude will make you attract the same kind of guys to your life for marriage and become a very powerful and fulfilled lady.

COMMUNITY GOALS.

Highly fulfilled ladies have community goals. The most effective ladies in history are those who moved beyond setting goals for themselves by setting viable and laudable goals for their communities. They are always making effort to make life easier and better for the people in their communities.

v   What are your community goals?

v   What do you want to be remembered for?

v   How do you want people to feel and act at the mention of your name?

One of the greatest things you can ever do to become a lady of impact and admired personality is to have great and consuming community goals. You must use your ideas, talents, resources, wealth, intelligence, influence and personal power to improve the lives of the folks in your community. This is one of the qualities that distinguish highly fulfilled ladies from the average ones. They are only thinking of donating something of great value to their communities. To really become a very competent, admirable, successful and fulfilled lady; you must have community goals. You must endeavour to use all you have gotten to make a significant difference in the lives of the people in your community. The good thing is that no matter your present circumstances and status ; you have got something of value to donate to your community. You have something to give to the next person you are going to meet in your life. As Mother Theresa, one of the most influential women in history once said, "If you cannot feed a hundred people; then feed just one". The little money you donated to a trusted NGO in your community can make a remarkable difference in the lives of thousands of the less privileged. That's why you must have community goals for your life. That's the only way you will become a happier and fulfilled lady.

BE ACTION ORIENTED.

It is not enough to set goals for your life; you must also understand all it takes to reach your goals and make unrelenting effort to reach your desired end.

One of the greatest qualities of highly fulfilled ladies is that they are always taking action to reach their goals. Highly competent ladies are always on the move. They decide on what they intend to accomplish in every aspect of their life; determine all it takes to reach there; and make a committed effort to reaching their desired end. Having developed a master-plan for your life; you must understand the price you need to pay to achieve all your goals and be willing to pay the required prices to accomplish all your aims. You must be very committed to your course and goals and make unrelenting effort to reach them. Any goal that is void of action is merely a wish; and would not bring any meaningful result. That's why you must be action-oriented and always taking steps to reach your true goals.

> If you cannot feed a hundred people; then feed just one
> ....Mother Theresa

PERSEVERE UNTIL YOU ACHIEVE YOUR GOALS

Another great quality that competent ladies possess that distinguish them from the average ones is the ability to keep on pursuing their goals despite mistakes, failures, oppositions, objections, mockery or challenges. They never believe anything is impossible. Successful ladies fail and make many mistakes in the pursuit of their goals but never discouraged from moving on towards their desired ends. Probably, you have had two or more relationship failures in the past. Maybe you had been faced with great stumbling blocks in your desire to get married and are about to give up the possibility of getting married. This decision and conclusion will never make you a better and fulfilled lady.

The best you could do now is to be very sincere to yourself; determine what had been responsible for your past relationship failures; accept responsibility for all the mistakes you've made in your effort to get married and make a determined effort never to make those mistakes in your future relationships. You must never be held back by your past relationships. You must be sincere enough to identify and rectify your past mistakes and character flaws and be enthusiastic about your future relationships. Most successful ladies that are now married have had it very tough in the past. Some of them had unproductive relationships in the past as a result of their flaw manners and factors that are under their control. But they just take a staunch decision at a point in their lives to forget about the past failures; eliminate their flaw manners and take absolute control of their future relationships and thereby got married to their desired guys.

> The decision and conclusion to give up
> on the possibility of getting married will
> Never make you a better and fulfilled lady.
> -------------- Festus Toks.

The past relationship failures can really provide some vital experience and lesson that will make you handle all your future relationships effectively and productively; if you really have positive attitude towards the future. That's why you must never be held back by your past relationships. You must be very optimistic about your future relationships. That's the only way you will cultivate the admirable quality that will make you a lady that great guys are eager to marry.

The quality of persistence is not a substitute in your desire to reach the top. You must be enthusiastic about the future and be willing to persevere until you accomplish all your goals. Highly successful ladies failed and make numerous mistakes on their journey to the top. Oprah Winfrey was fired in her first job as a TV presenter; but today, Oprah is the highest paid and the most popular entertainer in the World. As a lady aspiring to accomplish remarkable things in life; you must expect to make mistakes, fail or face obstacles and objection in the pursuance of your true goals; but must persevere to keep on moving until all your goals are accomplished.

Remember, success is attractive. When you are great achiever in your field; you will attract guys that are great achievers in their field to your life. When you are a celebrity; you will eventually court and marry a celebrity. Having goals, taking actions, and persevering to reach your goals make you a very competent lady. It makes you attract great guys that are going towards a greater height for marriage.

DESIRE A MASTERPIECE FOR YOUR LIFE

To become the lady that highly resourceful guys are eager to marry;
you must desire a masterpiece for your life. You must base your life, values and perception on your future aspirations. You must cultivate the attitude of self-belief, self-confidence and self-dignity. You must be enthusiastic towards your excellent future. You must never make yourself an object of pity. You must be very optimistic of a glorious future.
As a lady who wants to get married to a great guy; you must desire a great future, a masterpiece, and remarkable life and make unrelenting effort to reach your desired end. The law of attraction says, "Who you are is whom you will attract" . Great personalities will attract other great personalities. That's why you must desire nothing but the best in all your future undertakings.

> Who you are is whom you will attract.
> ------------ Festus Toks.

BELIEVE IN YOURSELF.
Having set remarkable goals for your life; you must believe in your abilities, skills, talents, knowledge and

intelligence to accomplish all your desired objectives irrespective of your present circumstances and situations. The ability to believe in yourself is one of the greatest things you can ever do to accomplish all your goals in life. As an anonymous author said, "*Self-trust is the first secret of success*". Self-belief is crucial to achieving anything worthwhile in any field of life. Most people have succeeded when no one believed in them; but the odd is five to ninety-five that anyone can succeed who does not believe in himself or herself.

Self-belief is the master-strategist for self accomplishment. Self-belief makes you to be optimistic about your future. It makes you face and overcome every obstacle, problem and opposition that may come your way in the pursuance of your goals. A great dream without self-belief will lead to unproductive, underachieving and unsuccessful life. Self-belief is the foundation upon which our lives are built. As the Roman emperor, Marcus Antonunus said, "*Our life is what our thoughts make it*". Author Claude Anderson said it more profoundly, "*The way an individual or group perceives itself is a critical determinant of their drives and goals*". It is your belief-system that determines your life-system. What you picture in your heart determines what you will eventually accomplish in life. That's why you must have a positive belief towards yourself. Positive belief leads to positive action that eventually give births to positive results. Those ladies that have self-belief in themselves end up achieving remarkable things in life.

> It is your belief-system that determines your life-system.
> ---------- Festus Toks

Remember, every great achievement in any field of life is

made by those who believe in themselves. Highly successful and fulfilled ladies never doubted their ability to get married to their desired guys and achieve remarkable things in life. You must believe that you have the amiable and admirable qualities that will make you the favourite of highly resourceful guys for marriage.

When you believe this way, you will begin to act, feel, and behave this way and eventually attract great guys for marriage.

BE A LADY OF GREAT DREAMS TOWARDS THE FUTURE

1. Have a clear mental picture of your desired end.

2. Take every step, action and movement towards the accomplishment of every of your true goals

3. Believe that you have all the knowledge, intelligence, ideas, capabilities and qualities to accomplish all your desired goals.

4. Be committed to excellence. Desire a masterpiece for your life.

5. Look at problems, obstacles and oppositions at the eyes and keep on moving towards your true goals. Highly fulfilled ladies overcome numerous problems to become effective in life.

6. Persistence is the master quality of human attainments. Resolve today to persevere until you achieve all your objectives and goals in life.

3

BE A RESOURCEFUL, PRODUCTIVE AND FUTURE-ORIENTED LADY

Be an asset, and not a liability to your spouse.
....................Festus Toks

Some years ago, I was invited to a singles seminar where the speaker asked those aspiring to get married in six months time to stand on their feet. To my surprise, I discovered that over 70% of the ladies that signified their intention to get married soonest are not productive or resourceful. Most of these ladies have no reliable profession, career or job that earns them steady income or wages. All they are concerned about is getting married and they never wanted to be productive in life. They have the wrong belief that the man should be responsible.

Perhaps, this is the major reason guys are not willing to propose to them for marriage. Most guys believe they are liabilities and highly resourceful guys will prefer to remain single than marrying a liability. Most young ladies these days pay more attention to getting married even at a younger age than learning, training or developing the skills that will make them resourceful and productive in life.

Most young ladies who would have gone to the higher institutions to acquire relevant knowledge that will make them relevant in life are more obsessed with getting married.

> Highly resourceful guys will prefer to remain single than marrying a liability.
> ----------- Festus Toks

The 21st century guys will do everything possible to avoid marrying a liability. As a lady that desire to get married faster, quicker and easier to your desired guy; you must be very resourceful and productive in life.

Most guys desire to marry ladies that will add values to their lives. They prefer to marry highly resourceful ladies whom they can plan their future together with. They want to marry productive ladies that will contribute, complement, and hasten their journey to the top. As the Old saying goes, "*Teamwork makes the dream work*"; and the best person you can ever team-up with in any endeavour of life is your spouse.

BE AN ASSET.

As a lady who desire to get married to a resourceful guy; you must be very productive and resourceful in your career, field and profession. You must make every effort to be highly competent, resourceful and become a peak performer and a high achiever in life. *Excellent ladies always attract excellent guys for marriage*. That's one of the fundamental laws of marriage. Who you are is whom you will attract. If you are a resourceful lady; you will eventually attract resourceful guys for marriage. On the contrary, if you are a mediocre and non-productive lady; you will attract the same kind of guys for marriage. When you are productive, resourceful and become an industrious lady; then you are an asset to guys. You have all it takes to meet your daily needs and will never become a burden to a guy in any courting relationship. You are in total control of your life. You can do almost everything for yourself. You can meet your primary need without messing up with guys for financial benefits. You will be willing to date guys for the real thing; marriage.

Too much demand on the part of the ladies on their guys has caused many courting relationships to end in a crash. Most of these ladies are unproductive. They therefore become a burden to their dating guys or any guy that comes their way. They cannot do anything for themselves. They look to their guys even in courtship for all their basic needs. Unreasonable demands of ladies on the part of their guys have ended millions of relationships in a crash.

Guys can easily be bored, discouraged or lose interest in any relationship as a result of too much expectations and demand from their ladies.

> Excellent ladies always attract
> excellent guys for marriage.
> ------------- Festus Toks

As a lady, when you are an asset; guys will be persuading you for marriage. They know you can add values to their lives. They know you have something to offer. They will take it as a privilege having you as their spouse. They will want to take the extra risk, go the extra mile and do extra things to persuade you to be their wife. You will become an exceptional lady that highly exceptional guys are willing to marry. Highly competent and ambitious guys will do everything possible to meet your standard, suite your values and convince you to be their spouse. As Winston Churchill said, "*My most brilliant achievement was my ability to persuade my wife to marry me*". Winston was a brilliant leader. Over 80% of Britons believed He's the most effective leader Britain has ever had.

He successfully led Britain to victory over Germany in a bloody war. But, Winston never believes all these to be his top attainment. He believed being able to persuade his wife for marriage was his greatest achievement in life. While? Because the woman was a very resourceful, productive, effective and highly intelligent lady. She was said to be responsible for most of Churchill's brilliant decisions as the Prime Minister of one of the most powerful nations in the World. That's why you must be a very resourceful lady. That's how you will ever become the favourite of highly effective guys for marriage. You must never settle for the less you can become. You must always desire and walk towards being the best in your field.

As I meet tens, and hundreds of ladies everyday of my life; I see those that will attract highly resourceful guys for marriage and those that will get it very difficult getting married.

Most ladies desire to get married but never pay close attention to building great and excellent careers for themselves. They have no career that earns them steady income. They believe that men should be responsible for all their needs and well-being. I have emphasized having a productive and resourceful career for yourself because I believe this is probably the major problem facing ladies all over the World. They all want to get married, but have no resourceful career that earns them steady income. Perhaps, this is one of the reasons they never get married or marry a non-resourceful guy. If you really desire the best in a marriage relationship; you cannot begin to live your life this way. You must be highly resourceful and productive in life. That's one of the ways you will ever attract great guys for marriage.

BUILD YOUR CAREER.

To become one of the most sought-after ladies guys are eager to marry; your career must be the ultimate over every other thing. You must be career wise. You must always think of the career you want for yourself; those that suite your values, and relate to your area of talents and gifts, and make unrelenting effort to become the person you desire.

* What is your career choice?

* What do you want to be known for?

* What are your gifts and talents?

* What do you intend to contribute to your community and humanity?

* What profession do you desire for life?

You must decide on a major career choice that suite your values, consume your passion and match your gift; decide what it takes to reach there and make a committed effort to attain your goals. As an example; if you have decided to pursue a legal career, it means you've got to spend some years of your life in a Law College. Most ladies have a wrong perspective towards marriage. They believe the only job of a woman is to take care of the children and never pursue any resourceful and income generating career.

This is far from the truth. As a lady; you must have a reliable career that earns you steady income for you and your intending family

CHOOSE WISELY

A career choice should be personal and not be influenced

by external influence. You know your values, passion, interest, and gift. It is exceptional to choose a career that suites your values and relates to the area of your gifting. As author Jean-Paul Sarto said, *"An individual chooses and makes himself"*. That's why you must be wise when deciding on a career choice. You must choose a career that suites your passion, interest and belief. As Dr. Mike Murdock said *"You can only succeed with an assignment that consumes your passion"*. You have the better knowledge of yourself. You know your area of interest. You know what you are ready to do at all time even without any reward. The great thing is that you have been equipped with great abilities and potential to perform at a peak in the area of your passion. The most frustrating thing in life is to be pursuing a career that does not consume your passion or make you a better lady. That's why you must live your life on purpose. Constancy to purpose is the secret of every great achiever in all field of life. That's why you must choose a career that suite your purpose, passion and values.

> You can only succeed with an assignment that consumes your passion.
> -------- Mike Murdock

ALWAYS DESIRE THE BEST OF YOURSELF.

One way to be a peak performer and great achiever in your career, field and profession is to always set a high standard for yourself and always go the extra mile by giving your best effort in all your dealing to always reach your standard. If you work in a typical organization; you must set a standard to always turn out good performance in your expected responsibility. You must desire the best of yourself, make excellence your watchword and always perform at the peak in all you do. One of the fundamental laws of compensation says. *"Your input determines your output"*. That's why you must always perform at the best in your organization, field or profession. Being the best always pays the best interest. If you constantly turn out great services to your clients, customers and business partners; chances are very excellent that you will become a remarkable career lady and become one of the most achieved ladies in your industry.

GO THE EXTRA-MILE

The best way to be a great performer in your field is to always go the extra mile and put the extra effort at delivering your expected task. *Only those that go the extra mile always have the extra hedge.* This is one of the most powerful laws of excellent achievement. Only few are willing to do the extra work, do the extra thinking, dream the extra dream and accept the extra responsibility and they are the most achieved people in any field of life. As the timeless saying goes, *"There is never a traffic jam in the extra mile"*. You must make it a habit to always do more than your expected behaviour and performance in any of your business dealing.

A little effort you put to your expected behaviour can lead to enormous and remarkable results. That's why you must always do more than what is expected of you. If you constantly do your best in your expected task to your organization and career; you will eventually become an integral part of the system. You will become indispensable to your organization and in your career.

The best is always in high demand. We all desire the best. Every organization desires the best employees. That's why you must make "excellence" your watchword. As a lady that desires to become a very effective, competent and highly performing person; you must always turn out great effort in your expected task and any of your dealing. You must make "excellence" your watchword, commit to excellence and always desire nothing but the best in all you do.

> There is never a traffic jam on the extra mile.
> ------------------ Old saying

ASSOCIATE WITH EXCELLENT ACHIEVERS IN YOUR FIELD.

One of the ways to get ahead quicker, faster and easier is to always associate with great achievers in your field. Their association can really make a difference in your desire to reach the top.
Every competent folk has gone to the top by learning from associations formed with other achievers over the years. Most Ladies have got married by just associating with other excellent couples. By learning and doing what others have done before; you will eventually accomplish their results. This is one of the iron laws of personal achievement and effectiveness. You must learn from every achiever in your field. Their advice, experience, mistakes and encouragement can make enormous difference in your desire to reach the top. Every competent folk learned from others before they reach the top. *"If you follow the track of a fortune lady; you will always come to a fortune."* The ability to learn from others is a rare quality that is rarely found in today singles. But, any lady that possesses this quality will become a very competent, effective and organized lady.

As a lady that desires to get married; you must endeavour to associate and learn from other fulfilled ladies that got married to their desired guys.

> If you follow the track of a fortune lady;
> you will always come to a fortune.
> -------------- Festus Toks

KEEP BROADEN YOUR SKILLS

To continue being relevant in your field, career and profession; you must continue to improve on your skills and broaden your knowledge. The ability to sharpen your skills to be better at what you do is the greatest thing you could ever do to ensure your continue relevance in your organization and field. *Those who know how will always be ahead of those who know why.* "How" is concerned about the solution and "Why" is all about the problem. Solution-oriented ladies are the most effective and performing in any organization or field and one way to becoming a solution-oriented lady is by continuing enhancing your knowledge and improving your skills.

In a typical organization; the three factors determining your position and income is your knowledge, skills and experience. KSE. But funny enough, your knowledge, skills and experience is depreciating at a faster rate. Most of what you know now will be irrelevant in the months and years ahead. Because we live in a very dynamic World; everything is changing at a faster rate. Most of your services, ideas and input will be irrelevant to your customers and clients in months and years ahead. That's why you must continue to sharpen your knowledge and improving your skills. You must keep knowing more about your field. You must keep improving your skills and knowledge to be relevant in your field.

> Solution-oriented ladies are the most effective and performing ladies in any human field.
> -----------Festus Toks

HAVE A FUTURE-ORIENTATION.

Most ladies would not date or marry any guy who is not very rich or wealthy. These kind of ladies don't want to date a guy who doesn't ride a car, or have enough money to meet all their expectations they desire to date and eventually get married to rich guys. They always turn-off young, resourceful and ambitious guys that didn't have the means to fulfill their immediate expectations. They have the ultimate decision to date and eventually marry rich guys. They are obsessed with dating rich guys rather than young and average guys with hope and aspirations towards the future. This decision has deprived many ladies of getting married than other factors you can ever consider. I have met countless numbers of those ladies that told they cannot date average guys. Their main reason of dating is the financial consideration of the guys involved. They don't want to plan, struggle or start small with average guys. They are more concerned with getting married to very rich guys that have gotten everything that makes marriage full, memorable and enjoying. This is how most ladies live their life. The horrible thing is that most of these ladies always end up regretting their decisions later in life. Whenever they realize their mistakes and decide to date young, average and ambitious guys; it is always too late to find serious relationships. Most guys will believe they have messed up themselves over the years and would not want to initiate any meaningful relationship with them. Most of these ladies always realize their mistakes and wrong decisions after they have passed the age limit of guy's preference for marriage. That's why you must not allow this to happen to you. You must be wise enough to learn from examples.

There is nothing wrong in dating and marrying a rich guy if you are fortunate to get one, but it can be dangerous and devastating when that becomes your obsession.

> The obsession to marry rich guys have hindered most ladies of getting married.
> ------------------ Festus Toks

One of the greatest qualities of highly fulfilled ladies that got married to their desired guys is that they have what I called "Future- Orientation. They have future perspective when taking decisions in the present. They know the essential qualities desired in a man of their choice and never allowed riches agitation discourage them from getting married to their desired guys. These ladies are willing to date highly resourceful, average and result-oriented guys even when such do not have much money at the present. Highly fulfilled ladies that got married to their desired guys focus on other qualities rather than the financial status of the man when taking marriage decisions. They are willing to plan their lives together with average guys that suite their values and possess all the qualities desired in a man.

> Highly fulfilled ladies focus on other
> qualities rather than money when taking
> marriage decision.
> ---------------- Festus Toks

A WISE DECISION.

Perhaps, one of the most brilliant ladies I have ever met in my life is Mrs. Chin Ade. She's highly resourceful, goal-oriented and very ambitious. She possesses some great qualities that are rarely found in the 21st century ladies that enabled her get married to her desired spouse.
Her spouse, Ade Bell is a very good friend, mentor and exceptional leader. Over the years, Ade and I have been involved in different projects with the Federal Government which have not yielded our desired result due to the mediocre performance of the people in our political offices.
. Our projects are very laudable, but the shady administration of the Government is always militating against the execution of some of the contracts. So, we were not achieving our desired results. Ade and I are very close chap and have consuming passion for our projects. We are both struggling to make ends meet, living on empty stomach for hours while working on our laudable projects. Most of our projects run into millions of naira but the mediocre system of Government is causing a stumbling block to achieving our aims. Ade never planned to get married in even two years' time by the time he met Chin because he was not having the financial ability to carry the responsibilities of a married person. But, all these changed the moment this highly resourceful lady came into Ade's life. Chin was a very resourceful, hardworking and intelligent lady that knows

what she wants in a guy. She's very creative, ambitious and has a steady source of income. Perhaps, she had studied Ade and discovered he has all the qualities desired in a man.

This accounted for why she was ready to get married to Ade even when he was not having the financial means to carry the responsibilities that goes with marriage. She knows Ade was not better-off financially at the moment but has gotten all the potentials to become a very wealthy, successful and fulfilled guy in the nearest future. Despite the fact that Chin had gotten other rich and well to do guys chasing her for marriage; she had future orientation and was willing to date the right guy that suited her values and would make her a better person. She was very committed to Ade despite his financial status because the guy possessed all the qualities desired in a spouse. Both couple got married in just six months of their dating. And in just one year of their marriage; this excellent couple are now living big. They now own exotic cars, have a nice career and living their dream life. They can afford to spend their honey moon and vacation in the finest and best cities in the World. They are now living a very prosperous, meaningful and successful life.

Chin Ade's future-orientation enabled her to date and get married to the right guy that suited her values, met her standards and made her a better and fulfilled lady. If she'd decided to date no other person than a rich guy; maybe she might have still been struggling to attract any guy for marriage.

The ability to have future orientation is one of the greatest qualities you can ever possess to become a fulfilled lady.

Most ladies that have dated and married out of lust have suddenly discovered that they cannot cope with their spouses after marriage and begin to have serious problems in their homes. That's why you must have future-orientation when taking marriage decisions.

* Did I really love this guy as a person?

* Does he possess all my desired qualities in a man?

* Can we function perfectly as a couple?

* Apart from his financial statue; do I really love him?

* Am I ready to spend my entire life with this guy?

* Can I really tolerate and complement his shortcomings?

* Do I really love him with no string attached?

These are the entire questions you must sincerely answer having future-orientation in mind for you to become a lady of admirable character and qualities that will eventually become fulfilled in life.

> Future-orientation is one of the greatest qualities of highly fulfilled ladies.
> ---------------- Festus Toks

LEARN FROM OTHERS.

Highly fulfilled couples started small. A recent study

shows that over 90% of the wealthiest couples started their marriage averagely.

They were living averagely, even some below average at the beginning of their marriages, but have great dreams, aspirations and goals towards the future of their marriage. Most of the highly fulfilled couples in history have no much money at the beginning of their marriage but had faith, passion, zeal, determination, ambition and a goal-driven life. But, today; they are extremely wealthy and can afford any comfortable home for their family. They can now afford to travel to the best and finest cities in the World with their immediate family for honey moon and holidays.

I always joke among my colleagues that the greatest mistake any lady can make is to say she won't date or marry me because I was not having much money. Thousands and perhaps millions of ladies have made such decisions and regretted their decisions later.

Dr. Billy Graham's first date refused to marry him simply because he was not having much money, but was average, resourceful, very ambitious and had a goal driven life. But, this lady had no future-orientation and unfortunately took the most regrettable decision of her life as she would later admit. Today, Billy Graham is one of the most effective pastors in the World and his advice has been sought-after by the entire America Presidents since the 80s. He's extremely wealthy, influential and successful. Dr. Billy Graham has been listed severally among the ten most admired people in the World.

As a lady aspiring to get married faster and quicker, you must develop the quality of future-orientation. You must be a future-oriented lady.

You must never be obsessed with dating a wealthy guy. You must learn from people not allowing yourself to have the bitter experience other ladies had had as a result of their faulty decision. You must learn from example. As Eleanor Roosevelt, one of the most intelligent ladies in history once said, *"Example is the best lesson there is"*. The obsession to get married to very wealthy guys has held millions of ladies from getting married.

Think about this;

* Bill gates, the World richest man's first date turned him off, because he was not very rich

* Warren buffet, the richest investor in history's first date turned him off because of his financial status.

* Billy Graham's first date turned him off because he was not having much money

* Nelson Mandela who is today the third most admired man in the World was turned off by h i s first date because he was not financially better -off

How do you want these ladies to feel now? Most of them will probably be regretting their faulty decisions. They just lacked future-orientation that would have enabled them to make a better marriage decision. That's why you cannot afford to live your life this way. You must not become a victim. You must be endeavour to date and marry any average, resourceful, ambitious and goal-driven guy that meets your standard and suite your values.

This is one of the greatest qualities you can ever possess to attract highly resourceful guys for marriage.

BE A RESOURCEFUL, PRODUCTIVE AND FUTURE ORIENTED LADY

1. Highly resourceful guys would rather remain single than marry a liability. Resolve today to be an asset and not a liability in life.

2. Make a resolute determination to pay all the price required to reach the top of your career.

3. Highly career-oriented ladies always attract resourceful guys for marriage. Make yourself a career-oriented lady. Make every effort to build a remarkable career for yourself and you will become a powerful, exceptional and fulfilled lady.

4. Make a career choice that suites your values, consistent with your passion and aligned with your inborn abilities

5. Resolve to associate with every remarkable performer in your field. Learn what they learn. Do what they do and behave as they behave.

6. Resolve today to be a future-oriented lady. Make every of your present decision based on your future aspirations. Be futuristic when taking decisions in important aspects of your life. Look into the future of the guy you intend to spend the rest of your life with.

4

BE A MASTER OF FASHION

**MEN FALL IN LOVE WITH THEIR EYES;
WOMEN FALL IN LOVE WITH THEIR EAR.**

---------------------- Paul McGraw.

One of the greatest skills you can ever possess to attract great guys for marriage is the skill of dressing appropriately, neatly, attractively, and nicely at every of your appearances and outings. Most ladies never pay close attention to their dressing at every outing, but *"How you dress determines the kind of guys you attract to your life*. As Dr. Umai Ukpai once said, *"The way you dress determines how people address you"*. As a lady that desire to command the attention of great guys for marriage; it is extremely crucial you always dress up in a way you will look attractive to people. You must be very cautious of what you wear at every outing; knowing well that *"How you dress have a telling statement to others about   you "* . Some ladies take care of their inner qualities but neglect their outer ones. They have good character, pleasant personalities and great virtue but never pay close attention to their physical qualities. These ladies pay very little or no attention to their dressing. Some of them even like to dress like married women. This single attitude can hinders you from achieving your marriage goals. To become the lady great guys are eager to marry; you must possess both attractive inner and outer qualities. Both qualities must be adequately taken care of. That's why you must be very concerned of your dressing mode at every of your outing. You must always dress in a way that suites the occasion.

> The way you dress determines how people address you.
> --------- Dr. Umai Ukpai

The ability to always dress attractively, politely, neatly, nicely and with sense of discipline is perhaps one of the greatest thing you can ever do to command attention in any outing and attract great guys for friendship and marriage. *Men are attracted to attractive ladies.* The statement you send to others through your dressing during your first acquaintance says a lot if that encounter will lead to a meaningful and desired end. People make up their mind about you during the first few seconds of your meeting and over 80% of their conclusion is drawn through your physical appearance. As Roger Ailes, the foremost political consultant once said, *"We generally make up our mind about people within a matter of seconds whether or not we're going to like them or even trust them"*.

Highly effective ladies that attract great guys for marriage are master of dressing. The conclusion guys draw from you during a first acquaintance determines what you make of those relationships. Ladies with poor sense of dressing are quickly written-off in a relationship. That's why you must always dress up nicely, attractively and beautifully because your dressing has a lot to say to guys about you and you might never get a second chance to make a good first impression. That's why you must always dress nicely to attract great guys for marriage.

MAINTAIN EXCELLENT PHYSICAL APPEARANCE.

Highly effective ladies try to maintain excellent physical appearance.
Guys like to be friends with ladies that are physically attractive to others. Study upon study have asserted the fact that people who are perceived as physically attractive are able to persuade others to give money, buy more products, influence more people and donate

in a worthwhile course than those perceived as average in appearance. That's why most organization prefer to use ladies with excellent physical appearance as customers relations personnel, because they've gotten all the qualities to make more sales, convince more prospect and persuade more prospective customers about the company's product than the average ones. Highly attractive ladies are perceived as more competent, gifted, kind and powerful than the average ladies. According to studies by mills and Arouson, *"Attractive females can change the attitudes of male more than unattractive females can"*. That's why you must always dress attractively all days of your life. Guys can inconvenience themselves to meet the standards of attractive ladies. That's why highly attractive ladies are more favoured, tolerated, pleased, and can initiate relationships with the opposite sex faster than the unattractive ones.

As a lady that desires to become one of the most sought-after for marriage; you must have a sense of dressing. You must always dress attractively and nicely.

> Guys like to be friends with ladies that are perceived to be physically attractive.
> ------------- Festus Toks

DRESSING OFFERS A TELLING STATEMENT ABOUT YOU

When you are in an outing, a social gathering or meet people for the first time; it is your dressing that indicates how you are perceived by others. The way you dress would first offers a statement to people about you before you even open your mouth to utter any word. The message your dress offers always determines the outcome of every of your dealings; be it in relationships, business or any other life endeavour. That's why excellent ladies are extremely excellent in their dressing sense. Because, it is your outer qualities that first announces or offers a bold statement about you before your inner qualities; it is essential you always send out nice and attractive things to people about you. I have met some ladies that possess some nice inner qualities and virtues but whose physical appearances are saying the contrary. Guys can easily write them off through their physical projection. This has held most of them back from getting married over the years. People perceive you by your outer appearances and qualities because that is what can be seen. The outer qualities initiate you to a relationship while the inner qualities provide the framework that sustains those relationships and ensure that it leads to your desired end. Violation of any of these qualities is the reasons for your frustration, mockery and failure in every of your attempt to get married. For you to attract great guys for marriage; both qualities must be well taken care of.

Today, there are millions of ladies that possess great and attractive inner qualities, but are unable to get married due to their unattractive physical appearance. They have extremely poor sense of dressing and this has made it difficult for them to initiate any meaningful relationship that will lead to marriage. These ladies are attractive on the inside but not attractive on the outside. They have all the great inner virtues but lacked the physical appearance and qualities that can initiate any relationship for the inner virtues to sustained. Since it is what is seen that gives room for what is not seen. Guys tend to write off their inner virtues based on how they are perceived on the outside.

As a lady aspiring to attract great guys for marriage; it is extremely important you take absolute control of both your inner and outer qualities. You must cultivate good manners that will make you attractive on the inside and also have excellent sense of dressing to always appear attractive in all outing, social gathering and everyday of your life. You must cultivate a neat appearance in every way, situation and everyday of your life from your hair to your toes.

> People respond 55% to your body language and expression.
> ------------Zig Ziglar

There is no substitute to attractive dressing and physical appearance for any lady that desires to attract great guys for marriage. It is the initiator of most kinds of relationship. Guys pay close attention to your sense of dressing.

Attractive ladies will always attract guys for marriage; because your physical appearance sends out signals to guys about you. As Zig Ziglar, the foremost relationship psychologist said, *"People respond 55% to your body language and expression"*. That's why you must let your dressing send out good impression about you. You must always put on neat, good, well-tailored, and fitting dresses that will show your beauty, physical qualities and uniqueness.

DRESS TO FIT; NOT TO EMULATE.

The common trend among the 21st century ladies is that they tend to emulate others in how they dress, act, speak and think. Most ladies emulate others in their way of dressing. But in the real sense, a perfect dress for a particular lady may be a disaster for another, because every individual has his/her own uniqueness. That's why you must always dress in a way that exhibits your own shape, uniqueness and makes you attractive. You must always dress in your own way and not in other people's way and opinion. The style that makes a particular lady to be nice and unique may not necessarily make you attractive. It is therefore advisable you always dress to fit and not to emulate. Self-knowledge is very crucial to having an excellent sense of dressing. It enables you to know how to dress and show your uniqueness. You have the best knowledge of yourself. So, you must always dress in a way that makes you exceptional, attractive and nice. You must always dress to fit and not to emulate.

> Dressing seductively portrays you as irresponsible to responsible guys.
> ------------ Festus Toks

HAVE A SENSE OF DRESSING.

Any lady who doesn't have a sense of dressing is doing herself a great deal of harm. A lady can be pretty and beautiful but without an excellent sense of dressing may not be attractive to guys. I can vividly say that almost 70% of my friends are ladies. In my life, I have associated with ladies than guys. During my college days, I spent a great deal of my time with ladies than with guys. This has made me discover a great deal of facts, secrets and information about ladies generally that I wouldn't have known in the absence of these relationships. I have met ladies that are not too attractive, pretty or beautiful but have a great knowledge of dressing. They had what I called "IQ" of dressing and attracted guys faster than those ladies that were pretty but had no sense of dressing. These average ladies are not too pretty, but know how to dress attractively and what to wear at every outing that will make them attractive to guys. They always paid close attention to their dressing attitude and got hooked to great guys for friendship. Likewise, I have met some very pretty ladies that had problem commanding the attention of guys as a result of their poor sense of dressing. These ladies don't know how to dress to exhibit their uniqueness, so they are often neglected in any setting for ladies that are excellent in their way of dressing.

Having a sense of dressing is one of the greatest relationship skills you can ever possess.

This skill can make you one of the most sought-after ladies that guys are eager to woo for friendship, have as a courting mate or as a spouse. Most ladies have this attitude of dressing anyhow. This attitude has held millions of ladies from getting married. That's why you cannot afford to live your life like this. You must have a sense of dressing. You must always dress uniquely, neatly, attractively and modestly.

DRESSING ATTRACTIVELY DOESN'T MEAN DRESSING SEDUCTIVELY.

The common trend among ladies these days is to dress seductively. Most ladies like to put on cloth that expose all or part of their seductive bodies. This act doesn't speak well of you. This attitude portrays you as irresponsible lady to responsible guys. We all know that sex workers have their own sense of dressing. Dressing seductively can portray you as a sex worker.

Over this chapter, I have talked much about dressing attractively, but I want you to get me right. To dress attractively doesn't mean to dress seductively. The way you dress can portray you as moral or immoral. It offers a great deal about the content of your character. That's why you must always dress attractively but not seductively. Put on dresses that exhibit your uniqueness, demonstrate your beauty and make you decent and attractive and not those that exposes your seductive body. To dress seductively doesn't necessarily mean to look attractive and to look attractive doesn't mean to dress seductively. That's why you must have an excellent sense of dressing. You must always dress modestly, nicely and with sense of discipline.

> To dress attractively doesn't mean to dress seductively.
> --------- Festus Toks

DRESSING ATTRACTIVELY DOESN'T NECESSARILY MEAN DRESSING EXPENSIVELY

To dress attractively doesn't mean spending all your hard-earned income on buying expensive wears. It doesn't mean incurring big debt as a result of your buying habit. Most ladies have the habit of incurring debt in fashion trend as a result of what I call "Emulation syndrome" They emulate their colleagues, friends and mates in buying all kind of dresses even when the income says it is not affordable. I have met ladies that always borrowed to buy dresses to meet up with friends' pressure. This is a very wrong habit and will never make you a very organized lady. The desire to emulate others in fashion trend has made most ladies to incur outrageous debt. Fashion virus has also ended thousands of relationships that would have ended in marriages. The ladies are too fashion-oriented. So, they want to buy all the latest style in town, and when they cannot afford them, they tend to turn to their guys for financial assistance for their fashion urge. Because guys are easily frustrated as a result of unreasonable financial demands or expectations; they always want to nip in the bud any relationship that is too demanding.

Some years ago, I met a lady and was frustrated in just one week of our relationship. She's one of the most demanding ladies I have ever met in my life. Everything about this lady is demand, demand and demand. She always had something to buy. She wants to buy all the latest dress in town. I was frustrated that I immediately ended the relationship. I am not surprised she found it very difficult to carry on any meaningful relationship and chances are she will find it very difficult to get married unless she changes her attitude.

Dressing attractively does not portray dressing expensively or to incur debt to make up your fashion taste. It only means dressing in your own way. It means to a dress according to your size and always put on dress that shows your uniqueness. It means to always dress to fit and not to emulate. I am not against having expensive dresses in your wardrobes. Of course, I love and buy expensive dresses. But, I am saying that you should not be too fashion-oriented to the extent of incurring debt or inconveniencing your financial standing to meet up. You must always dress according to your size per time. The basic fact is that it doesn't need to be expensive to be attractive or unique. That's why you must have an excellent sense of dressing and always dress neatly, attractively and uniquely in a way that suites your standard.

ATTRACTIVE PHYSICAL APPEARANCE ENHANCES YOUR QUALITIES.

Various studies have indicated that attractive physical appearance will enhance your capabilities in all your business, relationship, communication, career and negotiation dealings. One of the ways to fail in any kind of negotiation is to dress poorly for the deal. It robs you of self-confidence and enables you to have poor self-image about yourself. An attractive dressing appearance enables people to want to associate with you, boast your confidence and make you a person of charisma and winner in all your relationship. Over the years, various studies have supported the fact that attractive physical appearances boast a person's chances of peak performance and success in any life dealing. In every relationship of any kind, over 60% of dating and marriage decision are often initiated by physical attractiveness of the people involved. As a study by Psychologist J.E singer said, *"Studies at college campus proved that female students perceived by faculty as attractive receive substantial higher grade point than male students or unattractive females"*. A study by R.E Barber said, *"Men will reject women lacking (in their opinion (good looks, disposition, morals and health"*.

In a study by Brislin and Lewis, 58 unacquainted men and women were studied in a social setting. After a first date, 89% that desired a second date took that decision based on attractiveness of the partner. Physical

87

appearance contributes greatly to your chances of getting employed in a job interview, contributes to your outcome in any negotiation and determines your chances of getting attracted to guys for marriage. Ladies that always dress nicely, attractively, and modestly are perceived to be of nice qualities, intelligent, great character, attractive personalities, and have more respect and chances of success in all their dealings.

Even, married couples are often encouraged to always dress attractively to their spouse. It ignites the fire of romance in the marriage and ensures that it is a long lasting and memorable experience. Dressing unattractively can make the couple to get tired of each other. That's why an excellent sense of dressing is required for an excellent marriage. Most marriages have ended in a crash as a result of poor dressing sense of the couple involved.

> An average lady with an excellent sense of dressing will command more guys' attention than a pretty lady with poor sense of dressing.
> --------------- Festus Toks.

As a lady aspiring to attract great guys for marriage; you must be an extremely excellent dresser. You must also dress in a way that will show your uniqueness and demonstrate your beauties to the opposite sex. Guys can easily be turned off by ladies with poor dressing sense. Most guys are easily lured into a friendship through how they perceived you through their physical eyes.

That's why you must have an attractive physical appearance. An average lady with excellent dressing sense will command more guys' attention than a pretty lady with poor dressing sense.

DRESS TO SUITE THE OCCASION

One of the greatest skills you can ever possess is to know how to dress in every occasion. Highly fulfilled ladies are extremely excellent in dressing to suite each occasion. That's why you must have dressing intelligent. It enables you to know how to dress to suite every occasion. It makes you to know what to wear at every outing. Some dressings are meant for a specific occasion. A nice, well neat suite is suitable for a job interview, but the same is not suitable for an evening beach. Having a dressing intelligent enable you to always dress appropriately. That's why you must do everything possible to improve your dressing intelligent.

ALWAYS HAVE A NICE HAIR-DO

Perhaps, one of the ways to always look attractive is to always make a nice and fitted hair-do for yourself. As a lady aspiring to get married; it is extremely important you pay close attention to your hair do. The bible even says, "The hair is the beauty of woman". To command great attention among guys; you must always make a nice and very attractive hair-do for yourself.

It is amazing that most ladies never pay close attention to their hair style. They consider this to be of little important, but this neglect can hold you back from attracting great guys for marriage. Thousands of guys interview in various studies attach great important to the hair style of their ladies. I can easily be piece off with ladies with ugly hair do. I cherish ladies hair style so much that I have followed most of my friend to saloon to make their hair. I so much admire attractive hair do, and that's how most guys think about ladies. They cherish unique and attractive hair style.

To become the lady guys are eager to marry; you must always make the kind of hair that will exhibit your beauty, uniqueness and make you look attractive to guys. This is a little thing but mean a lot in your desire to get married. An attractive hair-style enhances the quality of your face; make you look younger and attractive.

> The hair is the beauty of woman.
> -------- King Solomon

HAVE AN EXCELLENT BODY SMELL

As a lady; your body smells can turn-off or turn-on people especially guys. An undesirable body odor will driven away guys from your life. A nice and desirable one will make you likeable and attractive to guys. That's why you must always use a nice perfume that will smell nice to people.

EXCELLENT DRESSING BOASTS YOUR CONFIDENCE.

   Being well-dressed boast your confidence in any dealings of life.
Several years ago, I decided to attend a workshop organized by one of the Federal Ministries in Abuja. I arrived few minutes to the commencement of the workshop; but I felt "like a shadow of myself". I was not myself throughout the workshop. I couldn't relate with other conference participants even though there was an interaction session, because my foot wear was not appropriate for the conference and I looked different among all the participants. As a result, I lost my self-

confidence, self-worth and self-values. I felt inferior to other participants. That day, I learnt a very vital lesson that would make a significant impact in my future. Being well dressed in any life endeavour boasts our self-confidence, self-worth, and enhances our self-mastery. It makes people address us respectfully, politely and with dignity.

As a lady; if you always dress nicely, politely, neatly, modestly and attractively; guys will have respect for you, cherish you and admire your personality. That's why you must always dress uniquely to attracts great guys for marriage.

BE A MASTER OF FASHION.

1. Dress for success. Make a resolution to always dress nicely and attractively. Let your dressing give an excellent impression about you. Look yourself in the mirror. Resolve today to always dress excellently in all your outings.

2. Always dress like a decent lady. Never expose parts of your seductive body. It makes you irresponsible to responsible guys. Highly responsible guys desire responsible and decent ladies for marriage. Be extremely disciplined in your dressing. Always dress appropriately and decently.

3. Cut your suite according to your size. Don't be fashion crazy. Never incur debt as a result of your buying habit. Resolve today to have sense of discipline in your fashion taste. Buy nice clothing at your own affordable standard. Always buy according to your financial status.

4. Make it a habit to always dress to fit and never to emulate others. Always put on nice clothing that shows your beauty, uniqueness and physical qualities. Dress according to your own way. Always dress to exhibit and project your physical qualities.

5. Resolve today to always pay close attention to your hair-do. Always do unique and attractive hair style for yourself. Attractive hair styles

enhance the quality of your physical appearance. Always make nice, likeable and attractive hair-do for yourself.

6.   Always dress to fit the occasions. Have a sense of dressing. Resolve to always dress to suite every outing. Look yourself in the mirror and ask yourself; is this dressing suitable for this very outing? Always dress in a way you will be appreciated and admired.

5

BE AN INTELLIGENT LADY

Beauty and wisdom are seldom found together.
------------ Patronius Arbiter

As a jewel of gold in a swine's snout, so is a beautiful woman who is without discretion.
----------------------- King Solomon.

The wisest King that ever lived

Some years ago, I attended a singles seminar tagged; "Beauty and Brain" organized for young ladies by one of the leading women development organizations in Nigeria. It taught ladies to be very intelligent, productive, have effective communication skills, and other skills that would make them resourceful in life. The organization teaches ladies to be an asset rather than liability in life. This Organization is providing one of the greatest needs of most 21st century ladies.

I have with tens and hundreds of ladies. I have done a lot of studies and researches and various studies have asserted my finding that *"Most pretty, attractive, and beautiful ladies have no or low intelligence"*. They have attractive physical qualities, but lack intelligence or great intellectual ability. A recent study shows that only two of every ten attractive ladies are highly intelligent, have intellectual curiosity or great-mind set while the remaining eight are non-intelligent. They have poor mental ability and reasoning. *They are beauty in an empty pot.* As Baltasar Gracian once said, *"Beauty and folly are generally companions"*. That's why highly intelligent ladies are the most competitive in the world of marriage. They are well respected, honoured and cherished. They possess the virtues that will make highly resourceful guys eager to marry them.

> Beauty and folly are generally companions.
> ------------ Baltasar Gracian

When I meet a lady, my first consideration is her level of intelligence. As a highly intelligent person, I don't like to initiate any kind of relationship with a lady that we cannot operate at the same mind-set. The quality of intelligence is one of the greatest qualities most resourceful guys desire in a lady that would be a marriage partner. They want to marry the lady with great intellectual capacity and high reasoning ability. As the American-poet Philosopher, Emerson once said, *"Nothing astonishes men as much as common sense and plain dealings"*. As a lady that desires to get married faster, quicker and easier to highly resourceful guys, you must be a very intelligent lady. You must be a highly knowledgeable individual. You must be vast in the world of information. You must be a very competent, effective and resourceful lady.

> Nothing astonishes men as much as common sense and plain dealings.
> -------------------- Emerson

I consider lady's mental capacity as one of the top priorities in a marriage decision. I like an informed lady and this is how most intelligent, resourceful and responsible guy's reason. King Solomon of the ancient history is the wisest and most intelligent King in human history. He highlighted the twenty qualities of a virtuous woman in Proverb 31: 10-31. These are the qualities that make a lady attractive to guys. Only a lady with great mental assets will exhibit the qualities that most men desire in a lady.

Home management is one of the greatest functions of the virtuous Women as highlighted by King Solomon. A dull and unintelligent lady cannot manage a home safely and securely. Only an intelligent lady can manage the home safely, effectively, productively and wisely.

> Highly intelligent ladies are the most
> competitive in the world of marriage.
> ----------------- Festus Toks

As a lady that desires to become attractive to highly
resourceful guys for marriage; you must be a lady with
great intellectual capacity. You must be a highly
intelligent and knowledgeable lady because knowledge
is power. An intelligent and knowledgeable lady is a
powerful lady. The good thing is that acquiring
intelligence does not have to be formal. Education and
intelligence are not the same. Most intelligent and
knowledgeable ladies have little formal education.
Intelligence results from self-development. It is a result
of exposing yourself to a world of information,
knowledge and learning from others.

> Only an intelligent lady can manage the home
> safely, effectively, productively and wisely.
> --------------- Festus Toks

Eleanor Roosevelt is one of the most powerful women
the World had ever seen. She possessed great abilities,
unusual intelligence and mental assets that distinguished
her from other women of her time. She was one of the
most admired women in the World during her lifetime.
She was actually the brain behind Franklin Roosevelt
Presidency in the United States. She represented her
husband in most political and public functions. As a
result of her intelligence; she was able to make Franklin
Roosevelt Presidency one of the best the US has ever
had.
Any intelligent lady will become "hot cake" for any guy
to marry. That's why highly intelligent ladies with good

virtues are the most competitive on earth. Because, they are very rare to find. They are ten in every hundred ladies. They seldom have marriage problems. They are the most admired in any kind of relationship. Highly resourceful guys are willing to move mountains convincing them for marriage. Ignorance is the reason for most marriage frustrations. Highly intelligent ladies know what to do, the quality to learn and those to unlearn to attract great guys for marriage.

Perhaps, you are a low intelligence lady. Maybe, you lack the knowledge and ideas to initiate any meaningful relationship as a result of your low intelligence. This chapter provides the valuable tools and strategies to become a highly intelligent and effective lady. The kind of lady that highly resourceful guys will be running after for marriage.   I have met countless number of highly intelligent ladies that are happily married to their desired spouses. Most of them are not too pretty, or exceptionally beautiful; but their mental ability, inner virtues, intellectual reasoning and core competence enable them to attract great guys, initiate and maintain meaningful relationships that lead to fulfilled marriages.

Years ago, I met an 18 years old lady by name; Angela. She was one of the most intelligent ladies I have come across in my life. Even her colleagues attested to the fact that she was an exceptionally intelligent lady. Though, I was not yet prepared for marriage. But, I felt like taking her to the altar. She was smart, reasoning faster, thinks accurately, a solution-oriented, well-informed, had great inner virtues and possessed great mental abilities. These kinds of ladies are "hot cake" for highly resourceful guys for marriage. She later traveled to the UK for studies and the next thing I heard about her was that an eminent guy was proposing to her for marriage as soon as she arrived the UK, though, her parents refused; saying she was too young and that she was sent abroad for studies and not for marriage.

> Highly resourceful guys are willing
> to move mountain to persuade intelligent
> ladies for marriage.
> ------------------ Festus Toks

BE AN INTELLIGENT LADY

"Intelligence" is a Latin word "intelligentia" which means the ability to gain and apply knowledge and skills. As stated above; highly intelligent ladies are among the most sought-after folks for marriage. Today, as never before; most competent guys want to marry intelligent ladies. What I am saying is that no guy desires a dummy as a spouse. That's why you must make unrelenting effort to be a very intelligent lady. To become the lady that highly resourceful guys are eager to marry; you must be a very intelligent lady. You must always search for knowledge and information. Remember, if you are not informed, you are deformed and it takes information to be transformed. That's why you make a continued effort to keep enhancing your intelligence.

Intelligence is pertinent information. When you are very informed about an area of life; you can never become a victim of that area of life. When you are very informed about marriage; you will never become a victim of marriage. You must make every effort to improve your intelligence, enhance your knowledge and refine your mind-set.

To enhance your knowledge; you must cultivate the habit of reading. You must always read your bible promptly, read other great books, attend marriage and self-development seminars and conferences and always strive for knowledge. A lady that has read ten books on the subject of relationships and marriage will have more skills, insight, ideas and intelligence on carrying on successful relationships than those ladies that have not read any book on relationship. Highly intelligent ladies know how to enhance their charisma, improve their charm and initiate a friendship that will lead to a courtship and progress to a fulfilled marriage. That's why you must make every effort to sharpen your knowledge and improve your intelligence.

Today, the ratio of ladies to guys is four to one. Every of the 21st century guys have an average of four ladies as friends and they will eventually get married to just one of those ladies. That's what makes marriage the most competitive institution in the world.

What's the marriage hope of those remaining three ladies? They will continue in the search for a marriage partner. That's why any lady that desires to get married must have what I call "Relationship intelligence". This will make you have the insight, ideas, and knowledge to initiate, sustain, maintain, and protect a relationship that will lead to your desired end. Highly intelligent ladies know how to initiate and nurture any relationship to marriage. That's why you must do everything possible to become a very intelligent lady.

READ EXTENSIVELY

Great readers end up becoming great leaders. Reading opens the world of information and lead to knowledge. Knowledge shows the world of possibilities. Most of human problems result from self-ignorance. As Shakespeare said, *"There is no darkness but ignorance"*.

Most ladies finding it very difficult getting married are not unfortunate or unlucky; it is as a result of ignorance. They just lack the knowledge to initiate any meaningful relationship that will lead to marriage. Most ladies finding it very difficult to get married are reaping the result of self-ignorance. You have bought this very book to know why some ladies are getting it tough to get married and also learn those qualities that will make you attract great guys for marriage. The best you can do now to achieve your marriage goals is to begin to apply the insights in this book to every aspects of your life.

> There is no darkness but ignorance.
> ---------- Shakespeare

Highly intelligent ladies read extensively about all field of life. They read every material on relationships, friendship, marriage, personal development, leadership and other subjects of life. Ladies that have read numerous books and materials on the subject of friendship, courtship and marriage cannot reason at the same level of intelligence with those that have not read any materials on these subjects. So, reading makes you a highly intelligent lady. It shows you what to do to get what you want. Highly intelligent ladies that attract great guys for marriage read extensively on the subjects of marriage, attend marriage seminars, and form association with highly fulfilled couples to learn valuable tools and knowledge of successful relationship. Reading improves your intelligence. As Eleanor Roosevelt, the woman who became the Chairperson of the United Nation Commission for human rights in 1946, said, *"Reading is essential if people were to reach greater intellectual attainments"*. Reading habit is one of the greatest success habits you can ever develop. Most folks believe reading should be limited to schools or formal education. But, this is a wrong assumption. Reading should be a lifetime adventure. Highly effective people in history make reading a lifetime adventure. Highly competent, effective, powerful and fulfilled ladies read extensively on all field of human race. That's why you must make reading an essential part of your life. That's one of the ways you are going to become a very intelligent lady.

Reading improves your understanding and it takes understanding to be outstanding in life. I already have vast knowledge of courtship and marriage even though I am still a bachelor. I counsel marriage couples. I give powerful insights to guys and ladies on taking an effective marriage decision. This is as a result of my many years of studies and researches on successful courtship and marriage.

> Reading is essential if people were to reach greater intellectual attainments.
> ---------------- Eleanor Roosevelt

Effective reading is the key to effective life. Reading enables you to learn from other people's experience, failures and success. Reading shows how to overcome imminent life's problems, challenges and difficulties. To become a highly intelligent lady; you must read extensively about all field of life. A recent survey revealed that ".The most powerful, effective, successful and fulfilled people in our societies read an average of 50 books on various subjects of life per annum". That is why they are always ahead. They accomplish things faster and quicker. They are the first to know. As the CNN's popular saying goes, "*Be the first to know*". Because they are the first to know the information; they always utilize it to their advantage before the general public is aware.

Remember, two out of every ten ladies are intelligent. Twenty out of every hundreds are intelligent and two hundred out of every thousand are intelligent.

These intelligent ladies always attract great guys for marriage and one of the ways these ladies sharpen their intelligence is through rigorous reading. That's why you must make a committed effort to sharpen your intelligence, improve your knowledge and always enhance your intellectual ability to become the lady that highly resourceful guys are desperate and eager to marry.

> Be the first to know.
> --------- CNN

STRIVE FOR KNOWLEDGE

Highly intelligent ladies are always striving for knowledge. They always desire to know more. Knowledge is a critical factor in the journey of success. Self-knowledge leads to self-power. As Sir Francis Bacon said, *"Knowledge and human power are synonymous"*. The quality of your knowledge determines the quality of your life. As a matter of fact, when knowledge is wanting, everything is wanting. Knowledge is the critical difference between highly effective and mediocre folks in all field of life. As Psychologist Joseph Addison said, *"knowledge is indeed, that which is next to virtue; it truly and essentially raises one person above another"*. Self-knowledge puts one person ahead of others in any endeavour of life.

To become a very intelligent lady; you must always strive for knowledge. You must never be satisfied with what you are, what you know; and what you have learned over the years.

Lifetime commitment to knowledge is the principal key to personal effectiveness and long time success. As Pat Riley, the NBA coach of the decade, once said, *"When you stop striving to get better, you are bound to get worse"*. Sandra Day O. Conner, the first woman Supreme Court Justice in the US and one of the most intelligent women the World had ever seen, said, *"Never stop learning"*. Highly intelligent, effective and successful ladies are always striving for knowledge. They are never contented with what they know. They have what I call *"Bias for knowledge"* They always want to know the relevant information, facts and secrets about their field more than anyone else. Perhaps, that's why they are succeeding more than their colleagues, competitors and co-workers in their respective fields.

> When you stop striving to get better, you're bound to get worse.
> ----------- Pat Riley

Self pride is the greatest obstacle to self-development. Most ladies believe they have known it all and never make any effort to upgrade their knowledge. Know it all never knows it more. Whenever you believe you know it all and never make any effort to learn or listen to other competent people's insight; you are bound to make mistakes in the race of life. The terrible thing is that knowledge depreciates at a very faster rate. Most of what you know now will not make you effective or competent in your field in the months and years ahead. That's why you must keep enhancing your knowledge, develop your skills and listen to the insight of people that are ahead of you in life.

Excellent and highly intelligent ladies are always striving for knowledge. They are always striving to acquire more knowledge that will make them relevant in life. They always want to know more and more and more. Highly effective ladies have bias for information. They always want to get access to relevant facts before anyone else and use those facts for their benefit before it becomes known to others. Because they are well knowledgeable and informed; they possess the skills, wisdom and wits to initiate, sustain and carry on any relationship with the opposite sex that will lead to a fulfilled marriage. They know how to influence guy's decision to their way of thinking. They have all the charisma that makes guys want more of them. They know how to turn-on or turn-off any relationships. That's why you must keep acquiring the relevant facts, skills and information that will make you a very competent and effective lady and thereby attract highly resourceful guys for marriage.

> If you want to fly with the eagles, you cannot continue to scratch with the turkeys.
> ------------ Zig Ziglar

ASSOCIATE WITH OTHER INTELLIGENT AND SUCCESSFUL COUPLES.

Association can be very contagious. The person with whom you associate determines what you become at the long-haul. The friends you keep determine the life you live. The quality of your association determines the quality of your life. As a lady aspiring to get married; if you initiate a close association with ladies that have no values for men, those with faulty character, those that are finding it difficult to get married due to their personal faults, or those that have faulty and broken relationships or marriages; chances are very excellent that you will find it very difficult getting married or to experience a fulfilled marriage. Because, like attracts like. On the contrary, if you make committed effort to initiate a close and meaningful association with intelligent and successful couples that are happily married; those couples that know and exhibit strategies for fulfilled marriage; those couples that are having blossom, blissful, prosperous and memorable marriages; chances are very great that you will eventually learn their attitudes, believe and cultivate the winning insights that will make you initiate and sustain a meaningful relationship that will lead to your desired end; "Marriage". As Author Andrew Croofts once said, *"Never be afraid to associate with the greats, they will only make you great by association"*. Zig Ziglar, the foremost American public speaker said, *"If you want to fly with the eagles, you cannot continue to scratch with the turkeys"*. If you really desire to get married; you cannot continue to associate with ladies that have no values for marriage or those that find it very difficult to get married as a result of their faulty attitudes.

> Endeavour as much as you can to keep company with people above you.
>
> ---------- Lord Chesterfield

Ladies who associate with highly successful and fulfilled couples end up achieving excellent marriage. This kind of association is what I will call, "Mentor-learner": association. These married couples with excellent marriages are ahead of you. They have attained what you desire to accomplish. As a lady that aspire to get married; you must associate with other married ladies that are enjoying excellent marriages. A word of insight from these ladies can actually be the turning point in your desire to get married. This kind of association can be the guiding light that will actually guide you to your desired future. You must associate with every married, successful and fulfilled lady that come across you. You must be endeavour to learn what they learned, do what they did that seem right in your evaluation in other to achieve what they achieved. This kind of association will enhance your marriage intelligence, knowledge, wits and understanding. It will show you how to initiate and carry on a successful relationship that will lead to a fulfilled marriage. To benefit much from this kind of association; you must appreciate your mentor, show them absolute respect, be teachable, accept encouragement and criticism.

ASSOCIATE WITH OTHER INTELLIGENT AND SUCCESS-MINDED LADIES.

Another association you must be mindful of is that of your friends, mates and colleagues. As I had said earlier; the quality of your relationship determines the quality of your life. You must be mindful of the ladies you keep. You must endeavour to keep those ladies that have great character, live uprightly, have attitudes and are success-minded. Wrong association can constitute a stumbling block to your desire to get married. I recently met some group of ladies that told me they are not bothered about getting married. They said they just want to have babies out wedlock and continue to live their lives. They told me marriage is not important to them. These ladies are not lesbians, but they doubt the chances of getting married to any man. A close observation of these ladies shows that they have been living a reckless life all their days. They sleep with many men because of the financial benefits, have poor attitudes, act immorally and desire instant gratifications. They lead their life as a harlot in the brothel. As a result of their way of living; these ladies have given up on the chances of getting attracted to any guy for serious relationships that will lead to any marriage. Any lady that associates with these kinds of ladies will learn, cultivate and exhibit these self-destructive attitudes, manners and behaviours that will make it difficult for them to get married. Thousands and perhaps millions of these kinds of ladies are living in our societies today.

They mess-up themselves with every man that comes their way, learn bad habits and have almost given-up on the chances of getting married. Almost all ladies except in exceptional cases have marriage dreams. It is the frustration from their way of living that makes some ladies give up on the chances of getting married.

As a lady that desires to get married; you must be mindful of every of your association. You must never associate with those ladies that have poor attitudes, self-defeating manners or immoral way of life. You must endeavour to associate with great ladies that are success-minded and those with good manners. Remember, the choice of your friends determines the choice of your life and friendship is never by force; it is by choice. You must associate with those ladies with positive values and have positive attitudes towards marriage. It has rightly been said that destiny determines our parents, but choices determines our friendship. As a lady that desires to attract great guys for marriage; you must be mindful of your association.

Life can be likened to a staircase; and the friends you keep will either make you climb upward or downward in the staircase of life. Poor associations will always results to poor life, and on the contrary, great association will result to great life. As the old saying goes, *"Iron sharpens iron"*. This is the timeless principle of life. The person you keep determines the person you become. If you associate with highly intelligent ladies that have good manners, live morally and have positive attitudes towards marriage; you will eventually become an intelligent lady and attract great guys that will woo you for marriage.

> Iron sharpens iron.
> ------ Timeless saying.

BE A POSITIVE THINKER

To be a very intelligent lady; you must always think positively about yourself, circumstances, relationships and life in general. You must always nurture your mind with positive thoughts. When you dominate your mind with positive thoughts; you will eventually unlock your mind to great accomplishments and become a very effective lady. Great thoughts always result to great life. That's why you must always think greatly about yourself, situations and your world. When your mind is engrossed by positive thoughts; you will act positively, do positive things, cultivate positive attitudes and eventually attract positive guys for marriage.

ATTEND SEMINARS, CONFERENCES AND WORKSHOPS TO SHARPEN YOUR INTELLIGENCE.

Great conferences, seminars and workshops enhance your intelligence, knowledge and understanding. Most intelligent ladies are addicted to attending relationship and marriage seminars and conferences.

They listen to many tapes on the subject of human relationships; attend every seminar on marriage and personal empowerment. That's why they always gather more information and facts on how to initiate and carry about successful relationship than those ladies that seldom attend marriage conferences. I have attended various conferences, workshops and powerful seminars ranging from the subjects of relationship to educational, leadership, spiritual, finance and marriage. Highly effective conferences provide the avenues for life-changing information. Thousands and even millions of ladies have attended conferences on marriage where they caught insights that made them attract great guys for marriage.

As a lady that desires to become a very intelligent person that will attract great guys for marriage; you must always attend great marriage conferences and seminars that will give you the insights for effective marriage. Today, it is horrible that some ladies attend conferences and yet are less-intelligent or have no positive results in their life. Recently, various studies have shown that only 20% of the attendees in most life-enhancing conferences benefit and experience positive results in their lives. Most conferences participants are there just to fill the seat and never to acquire the relevant facts, knowledge and information that will better their personal life. It is simple; these kinds of participants attend conferences with no expectation and what you don't expect; you cannot experience.

A recent study by Harvard University Professors shows that people who get the most of meetings, conferences and educational gathering are those that;

* Come with the expectations of great ideas.
* Take good notes and
* Talk with colleagues about what they learned.

Most ladies attend conferences never to listen and learn from the speakers, but to chat, have fun, take pictures and do other activities that will never improve their intelligence. The intelligent ladies that get the best from every conference attend with great expectations, aspirations, and enthusiasm. They are the first to arrive the venue. They always take accurate note. They listen attentively to the speakers and also ask questions for more understandings and clarification.

PRACTICE WHAT YOU LEARN

A recent study shows that almost 80% of conferences attendants never go back to their notes, read the books purchased from the conferences or listen to the tapes of the speaker. Most conferences participants after the meeting never take time to review and apply what they have learned to their lives and perhaps, that's why they never see the results they desire. Knowledge is ineffective without use. Knowledge is only powerful when put to practice. What you learn in any meeting can only bring positive changes to your life when applied or put to use.

That's why only 20% of most conferences participants get their desired results. They are the ones that applied every bit of insight and information learned to their lives. Most ladies are at the conferences to fill the seats and never to acquire the relevant knowledge that will bring about their positive results. They spend quite substantial amount of money to get registered, invest a lot of effort and time, but without any meaningful results because they never practice what they learned in those conferences. Highly effective ladies achieve the best from all meetings because they always practice what they learned to every aspects of their life.

> Poor association results to poor life.
> ------ Festus A Toks.

WALK INTO THE HEART OF MEN

The ability to work into and win men's heart is one of the greatest relationship skills you can ever develop. Highly intelligent ladies know how to walk into and win men's heart to their own cause. They know how to influence men's decision to their own advantage. The ability to influence man is a natural and inborn ability to all ladies but not all ladies can actually influence guys to their cause. But, highly intelligent ladies have never failed to utilize their personal attributes to influence guys to their cause. They can walk into the heart of any man and accomplish their goals. The ability to win a man's heart is perhaps the greatest skill you can ever exhibit in any relationship that will lead to a fulfilled marriage. As Lord Chesterfield once said, *"Men as well as women are much oftener led by their hearts than their understandings"*. Highly effective, intelligent and powerful ladies that initiate a relationship that lead to marriage are master of winning men's heart to their own cause.

To become the lady that guys are eager to marry; you must know how to walk into the heart of men. Every lady has the potential, but not all ladies know how to walk into the heart of men. To walk into the heart of men, you must;

MAKE YOURSELF COMPETITIVE;

One of the greatest ways to walk into the heart of men and get married faster than you have ever thought possible is to make yourself a very competitive lady. Let guys know you are not so cheap. Highly competitive ladies are the most sought-after for marriage. Most guys like challenges. They don't seem to appreciate anything that comes cheaply. That's why you must make yourself very competitive. One way to make yourself competitive is never to let guys know you are desperate to get married. Always portray to guys that you have many guys chasing and wooing you for marriage. To really become a very competitive lady; you must never be too demanding. Too much demand on guys makes you a cheap lady. You must maintain your self-dependency. You must maintain your self-respect. You must never be too dependent on guys. Too much financial demand on guys makes you a very cheap lady.

It makes them to take advantage of you. Guys respect ladies that are self-dependent and have self-respect. Guys respect very challenging ladies. They do everything possible to suite their values and make them happy. Some guys can even go as much as displeasing themselves to please a very competitive lady.

Most ladies believe the only way of winning guys' heart is through active sex. They believe if they are very active on bed; guys will like, cherish and eventually get married to them. This very wrong assumption has made it very difficult for millions of ladies to get married. One of my female friends was once a victim of this belief. She once thoughts the only way to attract guys for marriage is to involve in active sex with them. This belief held her back for years until she had a change of orientation. She recently told me that this wrong belief did much in preventing her form getting married. She changed her belief and begins to attract great guys for marriage. Most of the 21st century guys are gold-diggers. They want to dig your gold and be on their heel. One of the ways to make yourself a very competitive lady is never to involve in active sex with guys before marriage. You must do everything possible to be sexual abstinence in any kind of relationship. You must maintain your sexual dignity. That's one of the ways you will ever become the suitor of highly remarkable guys for marriage. Highly intelligent ladies know all these and that is why they always attract great guys for marriage.

> If you would win a man to your cause, first
> convince him that you are his sincere friend.
> ----------------Abraham Lincoln

SHOW ABSOLUTE RESPECT;

Men like to be ahead. They want to make the leading voice. They desire absolute respect from ladies. When you show this quality; guys will also respect you as well because respect is reciprocal. You don't get your ideas across through force or power; you do so through persuasion. I have seen many intelligent ladies that have persuaded their courting guys taking marriage decision even when those guys are not ready for the responsibilities it entails. Today, over 80% of marriage decisions are initiated and influenced by ladies. Highly intelligent ladies use persuasions rather than force, argument or power to get their ideas across and win their men's heart.

BE SINCERE;

Abraham Lincoln, the former American president said, "If you would win a man to your cause, first convince him that you are his sincere friend" Absolute sincerity to guys is one of the principal tools you can ever use to become their favourite and win their heart for marriage. As a lady that desire to get married faster; you must be a very sincere lady. Men will only deal with you to the extent that you can be trusted. Absolute sincerity to your man makes you the dominant person of his life. It will make him to always desire more of you. You will become the person taking the major decision. After many years of studies, researchers have found that over 80% of the decisions of the most powerful leaders, thinkers and men in history are determined by their wives. We all know that without Eve, Adam wouldn't have probably eaten the forbidden apple in the Garden of Eden. Highly intelligent ladies are very sincere in any kind of relationship. That's why they always influence guys to their own cause and attract great guys for marriage.

BE APPRECIATIVE;

Guys like to be appreciated. Most guys are on top of the World when dully appreciated by ladies. Their moral is enhanced, attitudes improve and self-esteem grows when praised and appreciated by ladies. As a lady who desires to convince guys to your way of thinking; you must always appreciate every good thing in guys. It boasts their ego and makes them want more of you. As Professor William James, the most distinguished Harvard Psychologist once said, "*A deep need in human nature is the craving to be appreciated*". Genuine appreciation is the great need of all guys. Any lady that can demonstrate this quality will definitely influence and attract great guys for marriage.

> A deep need in human nature is the craving to be appreciated
> -------------- Professor William James

As a lady that desires to walk into the heart of guys; you must always appreciate them at every opportunity. You must appreciate their gifts, abilities, time spent together and makes them special to you. By so doing, you will have the edge in every matter. You will become guy's favourite in all kind of relationship. You will become the dominant person of their life. You will make them never to feel all right without your company. Guys will count it a privilege having you as their friend, mate or spouse. In our World today, even from the beginning of ages, the absolute power of women is in control. Most decisions in all fields of human life are influenced by women. Highly intelligent ladies know how to influence guys to their own cause. Today, over 80% of marriage decisions are influenced and determined by ladies. The guy says he's not ready; the lady emphasizes why he's ready. As a lady; you can only exercise and exhibit your power through persuasion, absolute respect, sincerity and deep appreciation of your guy.

BE AN INTELLIGENT LADY

1. Resolve to be committed to excellence. Make every effort and pay the price to become one of the most intelligent ladies in your field.

2. Make a lifelong commitment to learning. Make every effort to sharpens your skills, improve your intelligence and enhance your knowledge. Be an exceptionally intelligent lady. Never be satisfied with what you are. Keep on improving your intelligence.

3. Resolve today to always associate with highly intelligent and successful couples. Learn from them. Ask for ideas and information on successful relationships. Appreciate highly fulfilled ladies and learn from their mistakes and successes.

4. Task after knowledge. Always attend seminars, conferences and workshops on relationships and marriage that would enable you acquire more insight, inspiration and ideas that will make you a very intelligent lady. Appreciate every effort to sharpen your ideas on marriage. Take every step to add to your knowledge and intelligence about relationships and marriage.

5. Always strive for excellence. Resolve to always go for the best. Demand the best of yourself in all your dealings. Think only of the best, act the very best and expect only the best. Set a high standard for yourself. Resolve

today to make excellence your watchword.

6. Always think positively about yourself and circumstances. Be an extremely positive thinker. Believe in your ability to attract great guys for marriage. Believe that you are exceptional. You are unique. You are beautiful. Believe that you possess the great qualities admired by highly responsible guys.

6

BE A CHEERFUL
LADY

Smile is the beginning of love,
---------- **Mother Theresa**

One of the most passionate and influential women
in history

Most ladies have this deadly attitude of always frowning at people. They are never cheerful or express the feelings of acceptance to people. These ladies desire a partner but their facial expression drives away all the potential partners. This is probably one of the reasons they never attract guys or get married to their desired spouse. The attitude of frowning can do more harm to your ability to get married than all other factors put together. Frowning hinders you from initiating any relationship that can grow to marriage. No guy wants to associate or get along with a frown lady.

I have met quite a number of unmarried ladies over the years and a personal observation shows that they have this deadly attitude of frowning. Perhaps, that's why they find it extremely difficult to get attracted to guys, get along with people or initiate any relationship that can lead to marriage.

> When the couple cannot laugh together, they cannot live together.
> ------------ Festus Toks.

FROWNING DESTROYS RELATIONSHIP.

The attitude of frowning has caused more havoc and destroyed thousands of relationships than any other factors. Frowning doesn't provide a conducive and pleasant environment for any relationship to be initiated, developed and nurtured to a desired end. When the couple cannot laugh together, they cannot live together. Frowning hinders openness in relationship and when the courting mate is not open to one another, the relationship is heading for a crash.

FROWNING MAKES YOU UNATTRACTIVE TO GUYS

No guys want to get along with a frown lady. The quality of cheerfulness is one of the greatest qualities every man desired in their woman. Most ladies keep frowning their face without consider the hindrances this can cause to their desired to get married. It will drives away all the potentials spouse and friends from your life and makes you a lonely person. The attitude of frowning doesn't welcome guys to your life. It makes you become an isolate person. You will become the lady that nobody wants to get along with.

> A man without a smile needs not open a shop.
> ------------ Chinese Proverb

Most ladies cannot just stop frowning. Every time you come across them, they are always frowning. They never exhibit a cheerful look to people. These ladies always get it very tough getting married. I can hardly get along with a frown lady. Frowning can cause great havoc to any relationship. Frowning can drives away customers, clients or target audience in any endeavour. The attitudes of frowning can hindered the success of your business, career or profession than any other factor you can ever imagined. As the Chinese proverb says " *A man without a smile needs not open a shop*" The attitude of frowning is a deadly havoc that will never make you achieve your marriage goal. That's why you must be cheerful to people.

FROWNING MAKES YOU LOOK OLDER THAN YOUR REAL AGE

I have never met a flown lady who doesn't look older than her real age. Frowning hinders your health, kills your body cells and makes you weaning and sickly. Various medical researches have ascertained the fact that frowning ruins health. So, frowning doesn't only hindered you from getting married, it can also have negative effect on your health.

A frown lady will always look older than her real age. Frowning kills your beauty. It ruins your physical qualities. It hinders and dwindles your wisdom and wits. Frowning people die earlier and younger than cheerful folks. The attitude of frowning is as deadly to your desire to get married as a potent virus. Frowning squeezes and roughens your face. It makes people find it extremely difficult to get along with you. Frowning also hinders you frown maximizing your potentials. It hinders and ruins your creativity, ability and intelligence.

> Anything learned can be unlearned.
> ---------------- Festus Toks

FROWNING IS A LEARNED ATTITUDE

Frowning is not inborn but a learned-attitude. Nobody is born to be frowning. The attitude of frowning that you have acquired over the years is probably the result of your parental influences, environment, self-belief, peers' influences, personal experience and orientation.

When you were born into this world, you were not born

to frown; you learned this attitude as you grew up.

IT CAN BE UNLEARNED

The good thing is that anything learned can also be unlearned. You can unlearn the frowning attitude you have learned over the years and set your life loose for a marital fulfillment. You can cultivate the attitude of cheerfulness and become the lady that guys will want to get along with.

Thousand of ladies have made this conscious decision to change from frowning attitudes,   cultivate a cheerful look and set their lives loose for greater accomplishments and marital fulfillments. They have made the resolute decision to change frowning faces to cheerful looks and begin to attract great guys that eventually hooked them for marriage. You too can do likewise. You can learn the winning qualities of cheerfulness that will make you a winner in every endeavour of your life.

CULTIVATE THE ATTITUDE OF SMILING

As frowning is a learned attitude so also is smiling a learned attitude. Smiling is one of the greatest qualities of highly effective, successful and fulfilled ladies that got married to their desired spouses.

A good smile portrays a feeling of tolerance, acceptance and provides a conducive environment to initiate, and sustain any form of relationships. A good smile opens the world of possibilities. As a wise man said "A good smile is universally welcome" An unknown author said it more profoundly, "Smile is the passport that takes you anywhere" The power of putting on a smiling face to everyone at all times cannot be over-emphasized. It can make all the difference in your desire to get married.

> A good smile is universally welcome."
> ———————— Wise saying

The attitude of smiling opens way for you where there is no way. It makes you a lady that other guys want to get along with. A cheerful lady is a winning lady. As Dr Akunna Uwakwe, the foremost psychologist says *"A little smile means a lot. It goes a long way to attract favour and make people have soft spot for you"*.

The effect of exhibiting a smiling look to people cannot be over stated in your desire to get married to your dream guy. Quoting Mrs. Oluwatoyin Oluwatowubo, the financial controller, Excel Energy services limited while sharing her marriage experience in an article published by Sunday punch Newspaper of May 21, 2006, *"When I met my husband at a wedding reception of my elder brother in the 90s, it was his smiles that attracted me.*

I so much cherished that, because there are some men who frown consistently. They are just known with that and that is not good enough".

> A little smile means a lot. It goes a long way
> to attract favour and make people
> have soft spot for you.
> ------------------ Dr. Akunna Uwakwe

To cultivate the attitude of cheerfulness, you must become an extremely positive lady. You must let positive things dominate your mind. Smiling is an expression of how you feel inside. You must be a very enthusiastic, positive and determined lady. Smiling is a winning attitude. That is why you must cultivate that habit to become a winner in your relationship and every aspects of your life. When you let positive things dominate your thoughts, you will think positively, act positively, behave positively and become a very positive lady and attract positive guys to your life.

SMILING INFLUENCES GUYS TO YOUR COURSE.

According to a study at Yale, one of the leading universities in the world, the professors discovered that "A smile is the single most powerful force of influence you may have on others" The power of influence is certainly the most powerful relationship skill you can ever develop, because smiling enhances your quality of influence. Guys can easily be influenced and get along with smiling ladies than frowning ones.

Any lady that can exhibit the quality of smiling will always win any guy to her own cause, achieve the best of any negotiation and become a winner in any endeavour.

In a typical job interview setting, chances are 90% to 10% that a smiling lady will be offered   the job than a frowning one. Most employers now consider attitudes in addition to intellectual ability in offering an employment. The attitude of smiling makes you achieve the best from any form of relationship. Smiling creates an impression of acceptance. Guys can go the extra mile for a cheerful lady than for a frowning one. The quality of smiling doesn't make you look cheap to guys, it only shows you are a pleasant, positive and powerful lady with attractive personalities.

> A genuine smile is the most attractive thing you can wear.
> ------------ Roger T Axtell

With good cheerful look, guys will like you, respect you, tolerate you, and do things for you that they would not do for others, even themselves. Guys can easily be influenced and turned-on by a cheerful and persuasive lady. As Dr. Isaac de clown once said, *"Laughter is one of the greatest mental tonics known to man and is the second most powerful human emotion an individual can express. The first is love"*. A cheerful look improves your self-image, enhances your personal power and makes you the lady guys will want to get along with. A cheerful appearance makes guys like you and wants to meet all your expectations. As the body language expert, Roger T Axtell explains". *A genuine smile is the most attractive thing you can wear"*. Guys can easily be influenced and persuaded by a cheerful appearance than by a frowning one. A cheerful appearance enhances your physical power, creates a conducive atmosphere for any form of relationship and increases your level of influence. Master-persuaders are very enthusiastic and cheerful people. To become the lady that guys are eager to marry, you must be a cheerful lady.

This quality will make it easy for you to initiate any meaningful friendship that will develop to courtship and thereby to marriage.

SMILING IMPROVE YOUR HEALTH

Various medical studies have asserted the fact that the quality of your cheerfulness determines the quality of your health. Physicians have agreed that cheerfulness is a great asset to maintain excellent physical health. As the timeless principle goes *"Laugh a lot and you will live a lot"* If you are always cheerful, laughing and happy, you will have an excellent chance of living an excellent life. Laughing reduces stress, improves your health and makes you a happy and positive person. According to Dr. Leland Heller M.D, in his book "Biological Unhappiness" , *'Laughter improves many aspects of the immune system, and it can make you a healthier person overall. Laughter also helps you to reduce stress, which can have a huge impact on your health"* Laughing is the cure for unhealthy body. It awakening your body cells, makes them at alert to face any symptoms of sickness and function perfectly and healthy. As the speech therapists, Mirtha Manno and Reuben Delauro, who manage a self-help clinic called smiling and health said, *"The mere gesture of smiling produces an electrical stimulus that affects the pituitary gland. This gland, in turn, releases endorphins, chemical substance in the brain that makes us feel good"*. Frowning does not only hinder your ability to get married, but it also ruins your health. That's why you must be a cheerful lady and cultivate the attitude of smiling to become a healthy lady.

SMILING IMPROVES YOUR LOOK

Laughing improves the quality of your face and makes you feel happy and healthy.

Laughing makes you look younger, feel refreshed, powerful and makes you a positive person. As physiologist Anon said, *"A smile is an inexpensive way to improve your look"*. The attitude of smiling is one of the greatest qualities you can ever possess to become the lady that guys want to get along with. It makes you a very positive, organized and enthusiastic lady. Smiling improves your look, enhances your health and makes you a positive lady. When you welcome people with good smile; you show you are a positive, organized and enthusiastic lady. Smiling exhibits your physical qualities and makes you a pretty lady. The qualities of smiling will make you become a lady that is easy to get along with; be it in your relationship, career, family, among your colleagues or in your profession. Most organization now prefer to hire a positively and enthusiastic employee to a frowning one.

As a matter of fact, the attitude of frowning can constitute obstacles to any effort to attain the result you desire in any aspect of your life. That's why you must cultivate the winning attitude of smiling. It will make you a positive, powerful, and fulfilled lady.

THINK POSITIVELY ABOUT YOURSELF

One way to become a very cheerful lady is to have a very

positive outlook to every event of your life. You must always think positively about yourself and the events around you. Frowning ladies are negative folks. They never believe in their abilities, talents, gifts or creativity to create the success they desire. They are very negative and problem-oriented people. But cheerful ladies are solution-oriented folks. They tend to overlook their problems and think in terms of solution. They never allow any problems to wear them out. They never allow any disappointment in any kind of relationship to deter their future possibilities. These ladies are very positive. That's why they achieve imminent results in every aspect of their lives. To cultivate the attitude of smiling, you must always think positively about yourself and any event of your life. You must believe in your qualities, talents and abilities to initiate any meaningful relationship that will lead to fulfilled marriage. As a lady that desires to be loved by others, you must first of all love yourself. As Oscar Wilde, the English poet philosopher said *"To love one's self is the beginning of a life- long romance"*. Psychologist Hicato said *"if you would be loved, love"*. Self-love is the key to life-long romance. You must have a very positive attitude toward yourself. As Claud Anderson said *"The way an individual or group perceives itself is a critical determination of their drive and goals"*. To become a very cheerful lady that will attract great guys for marriage; you must always think positively about yourself. You must let positive thoughts dominate your life. One of the fundamental laws of life says 'Your thoughts will eventually becomes a reality in your life". If you let positive things dominate your mind, you will eventually think positively, act positively, behave positively, and attract positive things and people to your life and become a very cheerful and positive lady.

> The way an individual or group perceives itself is
> a critical determination of their drive and goals.
> --------- Claud Anderson

SMILING IS A WINNING QUALITY

If your true desire is to become the lady that guys will woo for marriage; then you must cultivate the winnings quality of smiling. The bitter truth is that it cost you more energy to frown than to smile. It takes 72 muscles to frown but only 14 muscles to smile; and a smile is the first thing you notice about others. That's why you must begin to welcome every person you meet as from this day with a positive and cheerful smile. The political Consultant, Roger Ailes said, *"We generally make up our mind within a matter of seconds of meeting a person as to whether or not we are going to like them or even trust them"*. So, the first few seconds of meeting other people has a great deal of what comes out of that acquaintance. But various studies have shown that ladies that welcome people with positive and cheerful smiles always get the best of any meeting, appointment and all kinds of relationship than frowning ladies.

Ladies that welcome guys with attractive smile always end up becoming the most sought after that guys will want to initiate relationship with. That's why you must cultivate the winning quality of smiling.

> A cheerful lady always get the best
> of any relationship.
> ------------ Festus Toks

If you really want to attract great guys for relationship

that will lead to marriage; you must be a cheerful lady and always welcome people with positive and pleasant attitude. You must be a solution-oriented lady and have positive outlook towards every event of your life. You must always associate with positive people, read positive materials on relationships and always think positively about yourself and the events around you. The quality of smiling is one of the greatest qualities of every effective and fulfilled lady that got married to their desired guys. That's why you must endeavour to welcome people with good smiles every day of your life. It will make you a people person and enable you become the lady that others want to get along with, do things for or a forge a meaningful relationship with.

SMILING WORKS LIKE A MAGIC

Some years ago, I went to a particular Foreign High Commission to obtain a travel document. There, I observed an event that happened between two ladies and the office representative. The two ladies were both asking for a very difficult task from this young man that worked for the embassy; but the guy turned down the first lady and offered the service for the second lady. The first lady was asking with a frowned and negative appearance. Her frowning attitude probably makes the embassy representative refuse to offer the assistance for this particular lady. But the second lady was a very positive and cheerful person. She offered a nice smile to the guy, spoke positive things and demonstrated positive and cheerful outlook while asking the guy for this difficult task. The guy was so influenced that he rendered the service faster, quicker and felt happy for doing it for the lady.

Remember, both ladies asked for the same task, but while the first lady was refused, the second lady got what she wanted. What made the difference was the smiling quality that the second lady possessed and demonstrated to this particular guy. Both ladies were very pretty and beautiful but while one possessed the winning quality of smiling; the other was a frown lady. Smiling is a magic that will make things happen for you at a faster and quicker rate. A good smile will always turn away anger. It will make guys want to please you, do things for you and meet your expectations. Guys will always want to help you and make you happy. That's why every cheerful lady always gets the best from any association.

They are master of their relationship. They always win men to their own cause. If you really want to become one of the most sought-after ladies that guys are eager to marry, then you must cultivate and always exhibit the attitude of smiling. You must be a very positive and cheerful lady. This quality will make you initiate a relationship that will make you become a powerful and fulfilled lady. It will make you attract great guys to your life. You will become the lady that guys are proposing to for marriage. This quality will make you become the lady that guys want to get along with. It will make you become a winner in every of your future relationships.

BE A CHEERFUL LADY.

1. Resolve today to be a cheerful lady. Always exhibit good smile to people in all your future dealings. Become an enthusiastic lady and you will attract highly positive guys for marriage.

2. Make every attempt to avoid frowning to people. Always have positive perspective towards every of your dealings.

3. Resolve today to cultivate the attitude of smiling. Become an extremely cheerful and positive lady and you will attract positive things and positive people to your life.

4. Always think positively about yourself and the events around you.

5. Become a solution-oriented lady. Learn from every mistake. Always focus on the solutions rather than the problems. See every problem as a temporary detour.

6. Smile and talk to people. Become a very lively lady.

7

BE A LADY OF PLEASANT PERSONALITY

Politeness costs nothing and gains everything.
--------------Lady Mary Wortley Montagu

One of the most successful women in history

Personality is one of the various aspects of a person's character that combines to make them different from others. Perhaps, you are totally responsible for your personality. You can decide to be harsh, rude, headstrong and unassuming and drive away all the potential spouses from your life. On the other hand, you can decide to be people's person and demonstrate pleasant and winning personalities to people at all times in all your future dealings. You can decide to be friendly, pleasing, polite and attract all the potential partners to your life. As a lady aspiring to become the person that guys are eager to marry, you must cultivate winning personalities. You must have utmost respect to everyone irrespective of status or position of that person. You must be able to always demonstrate polite behaviours and care for the people you meet everyday of your life. To become the lady that guys are eager to marry, you must always show a feeling of total respect, responsibility, honesty, courtesy and acceptability to everyone at every circumstance. You must make yourself a pleasant personality, the kind that will want other people to get along with you.

CULTIVATE THE WINNING PERSONALITY

Highly successful, effective, powerful and fulfilled lady that got married to their desired spouses are simply ladies of pleasant and winning personalities. As discussed in the previous chapter; your personality can either attract guys to you or send them away from you. A person's various personalities are what make up his/her character. Ladies that initiate a successful or got the best from any relationship are simply ladies of pleasant personalities. Guys can sense their winning qualities and be willing to get along with them. To become the lady that guys are desperate and eager to marry, you must take the time to cultivate and always demonstrate the pleasant and winning personalities expounded in this chapter. They will enable you to initiate a relationship that will result to a fulfilled marriage.

(1)   Attractive: it means able to attract, pleasing in appearance or effect. Attractive personalities will always attract great guys to your cause.

(2)   Artistic: it means showing or doing something with skill and good taste. Any lady that shows skills at handling life's situations or things will always become attractive to great guys

(3)   Capability: it means to be competent and having a certain ability or capacity

(4)   Charming: it means to be delightful. It connotes to be greatly pleased and feel great pleasure

(5)   Clear thinking:- it means using clear thoughts or rational judgments about things

(6)   Cleverness: it means to be quick at learning and understanding things skillfully.

(7)   Courageous: - is the ability to control fear when facing danger or pain. It is the ability to forge ahead during the difficulties and challenges of life.
It means to be brave enough to do what you feel to be right even when the circumstances say contrary. This is the quality that separates highly effective ladies from non-effective ones.

(8)   Dreams: it means to be ambitions about the future. To desire greater accomplishments in life. Ladies who desire excellent achievement in life end up attracting excellent guys for

marriage, because birds of a feather flock together

(9) Enterprise: - To be full of initiatives. It is one of the greatest qualities excellent guys desire in a lady. Highly initiative ladies are the most sought-after wife materials on earth. An initiative and enterprising lady can make things happen, take a decision on behalf of her spouse and have the potentials to excel as leaders.

(10) Excitement: - To rouse the feeling of great emotion. It means causing great interest, feeling or showing excitement.
Exciting ladies are always excited about all life's situation. They are never discouraged from forging ahead in the situations of life.

(11) Gentle: - It means mild, moderate, not rough or severe.

(12) Good Looking: - It means someone or something having a pleasing appearance

(13) Imaginative: - It means the ability to imagine creatively or to use this ability in a practical way. This quality enables one to be good at problem-solving, solution creation and handling challenges creatively. But very unfortunately, this is one of the greatest qualities rarely found in ladies. According to various researches, only 2 out of every 10 ladies posses this quality. So, any lady that has imagination will become the person guys are eager to marry.

(14) Industrious:- it means to be hardworking. It is the act of being productive in ones field. Highly productive ladies always get married to their desired guys faster, quicker and easier than the unproductive ones.

(15)   Ingenious: it means to be clever at inventing new things or methods. It is the quality that distinguishes winners from losers, leaders from followers and outstanding achievers from mediocre ones.

(16)   Initiative: - It is the ability to initiate things or enterprises. Any lady who lacks initiative cannot manage a home or assume the position of a leader.

(17)   Insightful: - Is the ability to perceive and understand the true nature of something. This quality enables one to make sound judgment and carry on successful and fulfilled relationships.

(18)   Original: - Is the ability to be yourself even in difficult situations. To be original means to do things in your own style that makes you unique. We live in an imitation World.

Any lady that can do things or handle things originally will become a unique person and attract great guys for marriage.

(19)   Persevering: - It is the ability to continue steadfastly, especially in something or situations that is difficult and tedious. It is a fact that no great accomplishment can be made possible without the quality of perseverance. Successful couples persevered despite misunderstanding, challenges and seemingly insurmountable obstacles to make their marriage a success.

(22)   Polished: - It means elegant, refined and perfect. It is the ability to exhibit polished manners and a polished performance. Ill manners have destroyed many relationship and hindered thousand of ladies from getting

married

(20) Resourceful; This is the ability to be clever at finding ways of doing things.

(21) Tactful: - It means to have a skill in avoiding committing offence or in winning goodwill by saying or doing the right thing.

> An arrogant lady can never be loved.
> -------------- Festus Toks

BE RESPECTFUL

Respect is reciprocal. Respectful ladies are the most loved women on earth. If you examine the lives of fulfilled ladies that got married to their desired spouses, you will discover one quality they have in common; they are very respectful.

The good thing is that when you respect guys, they will also respect you in return. A very respectful lady will always attract great guys for marriage. The quality of respect provides a conducive atmosphere for a progressive relationship that will lead to a fulfilled end. As Cicero, one of the ancient Philosophers once said, *"He removes the greatest ornament of friendship, who takes away from it respect"*. The quality of respect is one the greatest qualities that is lacking among the 21st century ladies. That's one of the reasons most of them are having it extremely difficult to get married, because an arrogant lady can never be loved.

Respect doesn't reduce you; it only portrays you as a wife material. The kind of lady that will complement, build, be kind and contribute greatly to the progress of her spouse. When you respect guys; you boast their egos; when you boast guys egos; they will respect you in return, love you kindly and move mountains for you. They wouldn't want to hurt you. Guys can complement every other quality except the quality of respect. Respect costs nothing and gains everything. If you cultivate the quality of respect in every of your dealings, you will become the lady guys are eager to marry and attract great guys to your life. All these are the qualities that give you winning and pleasing personalities. The kind that make guys rush after you for marriage.

If you examine the highly effective ladies that got married to their desired spouses, you will discover that they always exhibited all or some of these winning qualities. That is why you must cultivate them to mould winning personalities for yourself.

BE A LADY OF PLEASANT PERSONALITY

1. Resolve today to cultivate the winning personalities of respect, responsibility, honesty, courtesy and acceptability. Make yourself the pleasant personality that will make others want to get along with you.

2. Resolve today to be enterprising, initiative, excitable, and industrious. Make pleasant and winning character the part and parcel of your life.

3. Be a complete respectful lady. Make a committed effort to show respect to every guys and people that comes your way.

4. Resolve to eliminate the attitudes of arrogant and pride. An arrogant lady can never be loved. You must be an extremely respectful lady to attract great guys for marriage.

5. Respect is reciprocal. When you respect guys; they will always respect you in return. Make a commitment to always show respect to people.

8

BE A HEALTHY LADY

Without health, life is not life. It's only a state of languor and suffering.

-----------------------Rabelais

Health is wealth! You've probably heard the line. Nobody can experience a fulfilled life without a sound health. Without sound and good health, nobody can enjoy life to the maximum. You need an excellent health to

*   Enjoy any relationship.

*   Enjoy your marriage.

*   Enjoy your riches.

*   Enjoy your career and profession.

*   Enjoy all your possessions.

As a matter of fact, the quality of your health determines the quality of your life. As Marcus Aurelius said, *"The happiness of your life depends on the quality of your health"*. To become the lady that guys are eager to marry; you must be a healthy lady. Health is the foundation of all human treasure. It takes a sound health to accomplish anything worthwhile in any endeavour of human race. It takes a sound health to initiate a friendship that will progress to courtship and then to marriage. One of the ways to attract healthy guys for marriage is to be a healthy lady. Most guys prefer ladies that look very healthy. That's why you must make healthy living your priority. That's the way you will ever attract great guys for marriage. If you have a sound health; you will enjoy a sound and happier life. That's why you must never involve in any habit or activities that will endanger your health and ruin your life.

TAKE CHARGE OF YOUR HEALTH

If you will be sincere to yourself; you are responsible for most of the health problems you've had in your past. Most of the health challenges you have had in the past are the express results of the destructive activities and habit you had been involved in. Most ladies have had three to five abortions as a teenager or while growing up. When they eventually get married; most these ladies always find it difficult to conceive due to their weak fallopian tubes.

It is a pity that most ladies never take the issues of their health as serious as it should be. They keep on involving in deadly acts that may cut-short their lifespan. We've heard that tobacco smoking is dangerous to health; yet most young ladies take a lot of pleasure in this destructive habit. Some years ago, I met a young Senegalese lady in the Federal Capital city of Nigeria; Abuja. And in just thirty minutes of our meeting; this young lady had finished almost two packets of cigarette. If one, going by the warning of World Health Organization that each stick of cigarette reduces the lifespan by two seconds, it means that this lady's life span has been reduced by 48 seconds. That's how most young ladies live their lives, smoking everything from tobacco to other hard and deadly substances. To become a very healthy lady; you must abstain from tobacco or any form of smoking. Smoking is harmful. It ruins your health. It endangers your life. It cuts short your life span. Most ladies that find it very difficult to have babies today said they used to smoke and were into drugs early in their lives. They are suffering from the express result of their smoking habit. That's why you must take proper care of your health. You must never involve in any habit that will endanger your future. That's one of the ways you will become a healthy lady and attract great guys for marriage.

> The happiness of your life depends on the quality of your health.
> --------------- Marcus Aurelius

DRUGS RUIN HEALTH.

Hard drugs kill and the so-called soft drugs such as marijuana destroy foetus and can destroy health. The US institute of Medicine after studying thousands of research papers on marijuana concluded that marijuana has a broad range of psychological and biological effects, some of which are harmful to human health. This is why most ladies that take drugs suffer from one drug-related health problem to another. They hardly live and enjoy a fulfilled relationship and marriage. They spend all their earning and income on deteriorating health.

DRUGS HINDER MENTAL DEVELOPMENT.

Ladies that are into illicit drugs hardly have the ability and capability to activate their mental power to excellent achievements. They fail to develop the skills needed for coping with problems, challenges, overcome adversity, facing criticism, surviving failures or handling success. Ladies that are into drugs hardly develop their talents, skills to be, do and achieve the best in life. These ladies always end their life in misery blaming other people for their misfortune. To become a very healthy lady and attract great and responsible guys for marriage; you must do everything possible to avoid drugs.

DRUGS RESULT TO MARITAL PROBLEMS AND BREAKDOWNS.

Several years ago, a study was conducted among 500 wayward children to discover what prompted them to such destructive, crooked and bad character and habits as a way of life. The study showed that over 70% of the children that are into drugs, smoking and excessive drinking said they learned these deadly habits from their parents. Couples that are into illicit drugs hardly enjoy marital bliss and smooth relationship. They always struggle to keep, protect and sustain their marriage. Drugs can cause a bleak future for one's marriage and family. It is a destructive habit that has led to the early end of thousands and even millions of marital relationships and marriages all over the World. That's why you must do everything possible to avoid drugs. That's one the ways you will ever enjoys a smooth and successful marriage.

MAINTAIN A HEALTHY ENVIRONMENT.

There is an old adage, "Cleanness is next to Godliness". Cleanness is a critical factor for a clean and healthy life. As a lady that desires to become a healthy lady; you must make a committed decision to keep your environment, surrounding and home nice, clean and healthy. Healthy environment attracts healthy people and healthy relationship and thus lead to healthy and productive ends. That's why you must always maintain healthy culture and environment. You must always tidy up your environment.

Highly healthy ladies make every effort to keep healthy environment and surrounding. You must always cultivate this habit and become a very healthy lady.

> Cleanness is next to Godliness.
> ---------- Old saying.

LEARN HEALTHY SKILLS

Every lady wants to really look younger than their real age. This is the ultimate desire of almost all the 21st century ladies. But after various studies and researches on strategies for looking younger and healthy; researchers have found out that;

*   Healthy thinking

*   Healthy food

*   Healthy exercise

*   Healthy attitudes

*   Healthy reasoning

*   Healthy imaginations

*   Healthy associations and

*   Healthy environment are the attributes that make one really look young and healthy.

THINK HEALTHY

Over the years, researchers have found that the thinking pattern of an individual has a great impact on the quality of his or her health. The qualities of your thoughts have a remarkable impact on the quality of your health. If you think positively; you will eventually become a very healthy lady. Negative thoughts weakens the body, ruins the bones, kills the body cells and harms your health. That's why you must always think positively about yourself and surrounding. A recent study shows that a person whose life is dominated with positive thoughts live longer and enjoys quality health than those that always think negatively. That's why you must always think positively and healthy about yourself. You must never allow your present circumstances to dictate your thought pattern. *All healthy ladies are healthy thinkers.* When you always think positively and healthy; you will eventually become a very healthy lady. That's one of the principles of looking healthy, feeling healthy and living healthy. You must always think in line with what you desire and not what is happening in your life right now. Always think about what you would want to happen and not what is happening in your life presently. To enjoy a healthy life; you must always think positively. This principle has worked for thousands and perhaps millions of healthy ladies and it can as well work for you.

EAT SMARTLY.

Henry IV once said, *"Great eaters and great sleepers are incapable of doing anything great"*. Overweight is one of the leading worries for the 21st century ladies. Every lady desires to look slim and attractive. As a matter of fact, fat ladies are ridiculed and assumed unattractive in most developed nations. The fact is that most ladies are overweight as an express result of their eating habit. They cannot just take their eyes off anything eatable.

They have no sense of control and discipline over their eating habit. They have what I call "Eating virus". As a lady that aspires to look and keep healthy shape; you must exercise absolute control over your eating habit. You must make every effort to watch and keep your weight in perfect and healthy look. Most of the foods we eat today contain too much fact that can lead to obesity. Yet, most ladies are obsessed with eating without control. They eat all the times even when they are not really hungry. Too much eating is a self-destructive habit. Obesity is self-caused and it can also be self-avoided by any smart lady. The agitation to look slim at all times has endangered the lives of millions of ladies. But, I strongly believe that prevention is far better than cure in the World of obesity. It is better to prevent this one of the greatest problems of the 21st century than spending much money, energy, time and stress curing the disease. One way to prevent obesity is by exercising absolute control over your eating habit. You must have a sense of discipline over your eating habit. Eat as a result of necessity and not for fun. Eat nice and highly hygienic food that will keep your health in perfect and excellent condition. Always eat good food that will enhance your health values. You must have timing on your eating habit. Eat to stay alive and not everything you see. You must always eat supplement food that will make you live longer, feel better and look healthy. You must exercise absolute control on your eating habit. That's the only way you will control obesity and become a healthy lady.

Great eaters and great sleepers are incapable of doing anything great.
---------------- Henry IV.

HAVE A DAILY EXERCISE.

Daily exercise is critical to healthy living. Exercise is to the body what air is to life. Daily exercise keeps you fit, stronger, smarter and healthier. Early morning exercise which can take the form of any physical activities makes you feel better, and look healthier. That's why you must always exercise daily to keep fit and put your body in perfect shape. Some physical activities early in the morning or late in the night can form the exercise that will make you a very healthy lady. A daily walk down the street very early in the morning can make you fit physically and make you a very healthy lady. Too much rest and relaxation can harm your health. The body needs small amount of stress and pressure for your bones, cells and nutrients to be awakens and be in perfect condition. Daily activities and exercises will keep you fit, strong and contribute greatly to your physical well-being. You must engage in it to become a very healthy lady.

SLEEP SMARTLY

Sleeping is essential to good and healthy living. But, you must exercise control over your sleeping habit as too much sleep can ruin your health.
Scientific studies say 8 hours of sleep per day is enough to keep the body in a perfect condition and maintain good health. As a lady that desires to enjoy a healthy living; you must always have the required sleep after your daily activities and responsibilities. It is also essential that you exercise absolute control over your sleeping habit. Sleeping enhances your health and makes your body fit and refreshed. That's why you must always have a perfect sleep to keep your health in a perfect condition.

LAUGH A LOT

There is an old saying, *"If you laugh a lot, you will live long"*. The wisest king who ever lived, King Solomon said, *"A cheerful heart is a good medicine"*. Healthy ladies are very cheerful ladies. Happy people are always healthy people. Laughing and cheerfulness is very essential for healthy living. As Joseph Addison said, *"Health and cheerfulness beget each other"*. Laughter excites your bones, cells and keeps you healthy. Those who laugh long end up living long. That's one of the secrets of highly healthy ladies. They are very enthusiastic, exciting, revealing, lively and happy. Frowning ladies are the most folks with health challenges. The attitude of frowning constitutes great obstacle to your health and general well-being. That's why you must be a very exciting, cheerful and lively lady. That's the way you will become a very healthy lady.

> A cheerful heart is a good medicine.
> ------- King Solomon.

BE A HEALTHY LADY

1. Highly healthy ladies attract great and healthy guys for marriage. Resolve today to make every effort to improve the quality of your health. When you improve the quality of your health; you eventually improve the quality of your life and become a more fulfilled lady.

2. Health is the greatest blessing of human. Without a sound health; life is a struggle. Resolve today to begin to think excellently about every aspect of your life. Positive thoughts improve the quality of your health. That's why highly healthy ladies are extremely positive thinkers. When you cultivate these habits, you will eventually become a very healthy lady, attract healthy guys for marriage and become a fulfilled lady.

3. Resolve today that you will never involve in any habit that can endanger your health. Abstain from hard drugs, cigarette or any other substances that can endanger your health. Hard drugs hinder your spiritual, mental, psychological, and physical development. Highly healthy ladies never involve in hard drugs or other harmful substances. Make a committed effort to free your life from hard substances and be in charge of your health. You will eventually become a healthy and fulfilled lady.

4. Resolve to always have daily physical exercise. Make a committed effort to engage

in physical activities early in the morning and late in the night to improve the quality of your health. Daily exercise refreshes your body, excite your bones, awakens your body cells and improve your physical well-being. Begin today to exercise daily and you will become a very healthy lady.

5.   Take absolute charge over your weight. Resolve to eat smartly and wisely. Have a sense of control on your eating habit. Eat to stay alive and improve the quality of your health. Obesity is self-caused and can as well be self-avoided. That's why you must exercise absolute control over your health and becomes a fit and healthy lady.

6.   Make every effort to maintain a healthy environment. Healthy and clean environment is the foundation for a clean and healthy life. Highly healthy ladies maintain healthy environment. They are always tiding up their surroundings. Cultivate this habit today and become a very healthy lady

9

BE A MASTER OF YOURSELF.

(THE QUALITY OF SELF-MASTERY)

The first and best victory is to conquer self.
-----------Plato

BE A MASTER OF YOURSELF

Self-mastery is the ability to exercise control over how you think, act, feel, dress and all you do. The quality of self-mastery is one of the greatest qualities of every effective, powerful, married and fulfilled lady. A lady that lacks self-control is heading for a ruin. If you really want to attract great guys for marriage, then you must be able to put your taste, desire, emotions, ego, feeling, and thinking under control and be a master of yourself.

> A lady that lacks self-control is heading for a ruin.
> ------------- Festus Toks

The quality of self-mastery will make you a very organized, competent, powerful,
influential and attractive lady. It will put your personality online and make you a much desired lady. This quality will also make you a very focused person as lack of focus is one of the essential qualities of mediocre life. To cultivate the quality of self-mastery, you must have a;

Sense of Order.
It is the ability to do things orderly. It is the ability to think orderly, live orderly, act orderly, and be a person of order in all you do. Sense of order will put your life on course. It will make you a very organized and effective lady.

Sense of Discipline
It is the ability to be obedient and have a sense of control. The quality of obedience is perhaps one of the greatest qualities you can ever possess to attract great guys for marriage. It doesn't matter what you, who you or where

156

you are, if you are not an obedient lady, getting married is going to be a very difficult adventure for you.

Sense of discipline will make you a lady of self-mastery. It enables you to act, think, and behave according to your values, passion and standards.

Sense of Principles

A person without principles is heading for doom. A principled lady always moves ahead fester, and gets things done quicker than those without a principle. Sense of principle will make you a very focused, organized, effective, competent and fulfilled lady. It makes you to always want to work towards those things that give you joy, happiness and fullness.

Sense of Direction

It enables you to work towards your pre-determined goals in life. A life without a direction can never accomplish any meaningful thing. Direction provides the channel to your desired end. It puts your life on course. A lady with sense of direction will accomplish things faster than those that are living without a direction or meaninglessly. A sense of direction gives meaning to your life. It makes you focus on your true goals as a priority over every other activity in life. This is one of the qualities of every effective and fulfilled lady. They are always working towards those things that give them passion and make them a very fulfilled person.

By giving your life a direction; you become a very competent and organized lady. Sense of direction makes you to work towards your passion, values and interest. It makes you discover your purpose and make unrelenting effort to reach your destination in life. It gives your life a greater meaning and makes you a lady of impact. When you give your life a direction, you give your life a meaning and thus makes great impact and results to fulfilled life.

The most frustrating thing is live life without a meaning. That's the characteristic of average people, non-achievers and mediocre folks. They never give meaning and purpose to their lives. Sense of direction gives meaning to your life because you are going towards a pre-conceived and pre-determined end. Sense of direction makes you to forget instant gratification for delay and everlasting gratification. It makes you to forget immediate pleasure or enjoyment that can not stand the test of time for a more delay and memorable pleasure. Sense of direction makes you focus on your true goals and not on obstacles or distraction that may want to hinder you. Sense of direction also prevents you from cutting corners or involving in any crooked activities that may hinder you from getting to your desired end. A friend of mine, Efe T is perhaps one of the most focused, intelligent, organized and effective ladies in Nigeria.

She once had all the opportunities to cut corners and have $4000 in her pocket in a relationship with an American citizen. Despite the fact that she's from a third World Nation, and being a student that was not having much money in her account, she refused to involve in this dubious act. As a young lady, $4,000 would have meant a lot to her life if one considers the poor value of Nigerian currency to the U.S dollar, but, she refused to cut corners. She said she intended to become the first Female Governor of her State (Delta) and so cannot tarnish her name and image with $4,000. What a visionary decision! Efe T is a master of her life. She has a great sense of direction, sense of meaning and sense of goals that can be compared to known.

She focuses on her life's goals and not on the obstacles or immediate pleasure that may hinder her. I have no doubt she's going to become a winner in life. She will definitely become the first female Governor of Delta state and one of the most effective leaders from the large continent of Africa.

Sense of Association

As discussed in the foregone chapter; as a lady aspiring to get married; you must be mindful of your association. It is not all association that will make you accomplish your true goals. To be a very competent and effective lady, you must have a sense of association. Some association will only hinder your chances of getting married. Author George Pettie once said, "It is better to be alone than in ill company". Every ill company will jeopardize your chances of getting married. That's why you must have a sense of Association.

You must endeavour to associate with successful and fulfilled couples. As a lady aspiring to get married, you must learn from every successful couple you know. Relate with them, learn from them, act, behave and emulate every of their positive habits.

Be a master of your Anger

To actually exhibit the quality of self-mastery and become the kind of lady that will attract resourceful guys for marriage, you must put the emotion of anger under control. Anger will put-off every of your effort to get married. An angry lady can never be loved nor carry-on a successful relationship. No guy would want to associate with an angry or irritable lady. As King Solomon of the ancient Israel warned, 'It's better to be alone in the wilderness, than with a contentious and angry woman in a mansion"

> Anger is just one letter short of danger.
> ------------ professor John Hagee

The ability to put your anger under control is one of the greatest things you can ever do to become the most sought-after lady for marriage. Though, some events or activities may want you to get angry, but you must always put your anger under control. That's the only way you are going to become an admired lady. The emotion of anger will only worsen your chances of getting attracted to guys. It can even destroy all your relationships. As professor John Hagee said *"Anger is just one letter short of danger"* A wise man said it more profoundly, *"Anger gets us into trouble, pride keeps us there"*.

Anger makes you a slave

Another fact you should know is that anytime you are angered by a person; you become a slave to that person. That person controls your thinking, action, emotion and attitude for that moment. That person shapes your life for that very period. As John Hagee said *"Anyone who angers you conquers you"* King Solomon, the wisest king who ever lived said, *"Angers rest in the bosom of fools"*. So anytime you get angry, you become a very foolish folk. To really be a master of your life, you must put anger under your control. The emotion of anger has made many ladies lose business deals, relationships and many opportunities that would have benefited their lives. That's why you must put anger under your control. That's one of the ways you are going to become a very organized, powerful and admired lady and attract great guys for marriage.

> It's better to be alone in the wilderness, than with a
> contentious and angry woman in a mansion
> ----------------- King Solomon

Anger leads to personal destruction

Anything done in anger will always lead to negative
result and can hinder the progress you desire in any
aspect of your life. I have seen some couples that when
having little misunderstanding will get angry to the
extent of destroying their personal properties, effects and
possessions. I recently heard of a lady that got angry to
the extent of pouring a very hot water on her spouse. This
is personal madness. As Psychologist Horace said,
*"Anger is a momentary madness, so control your
passion or it will control you"* Anger always leads to
destruction. The horrible thing is that after the damage
and destruction have happened; those folks will begin to
regret every bit of their action.

It is better to be alone than marrying a very
temperamental lady. That's why an angry lady will
always find it extremely difficult to get married. To really
become an attractive lady that guys will woo for
marriage, you must always put anger under control. You
must never allow any circumstances or situations to
make you lose your emotion or self-control.

> Anger is never without reason,
> but seldom with a good reason.
> ---------- Benjamin Franklin

Cure for Anger

The ability to be a master of anger is one of the greatest

things you can ever do to become a very organized, effective, competent, and admired lady. This quality will single you out of millions of ladies because most ladies are easily angered.

To always remain calm and silence are the greatest cure to anger. Whenever you are angered and feel like reacting, just think twice and remain calm, cool and silence. In just a matter of minutes, your anger will die-off and you will become a very competent lady. As a wise man said *"The greatest enemy of anger is delay"*. Whenever you delay a reaction to the emotion of anger; you become a master of yourself and your anger will be subjected to control. It is better to delay a reaction to anger than acting immediately and begin to regret your action later. The greatest mistakes of life are made when one is angry. That's why it's not good to take decision while angry, act in anger, or respond to a situation or circumstances in anger. It will only make you to act foolishly. Delay is the cure to anger. Whenever you are offended, take it easy, cool, be silence and delay your reaction and you will become a very competent, powerful and master of your emotion.

Be a master of your thinking

As a lady that desires to take absolute control of your life; you must exercise absolute control on your thinking, because your thought pattern always ends in creating your life pattern. Highly competent ladies are always thinking on the changes they desire to happen in their lives. They think on the kinds of house they want to live, the kind of car they want to drive, and the kind of husband they desire as a spouse. The ancient thinker, Horace, said, *'Rule your mind or it will rule you"*. One way to have absolute rule on your mind is to think constantly on what you want in life and not what your circumstances is saying. When you think like a successful lady, you eventually become a successful lady. As Buddha, the foremost philosopher said, *"We are what we think. All that we are arise with our thoughts. With our thoughts, we make our world"*. Nothing is as powerful as your thoughts in creating your future. That's why Marcus Aurelines Antoninus, the Roman emperor and philosopher once said, 'Your life is an expression of all your thoughts". To become a very competent and fulfilled lady, you must be a master of your thought. Think in terms of what you really want to happen in your life and not the current happenings in your situations. If you really want to get married to your desired guy, you must begin to form the image of that person in your mind. Think as if you have already met the guy, think as if you and the guy have finalized the marriage arrangement. Begin to think as if you and that person are already married and about to go for the honey moon. If you really begin to think this way, in no time you will begin to come across the kind of guy you formed in your mind. It will become a practical experience in your life. You will begin to attract great guys, court great guys and eventually get married to the guy that meet your standard, suite your values and make you a very powerful, effective and fulfilled lady.

Be a master of your words
Another way you can exercise absolute control over your

163

life is to be a master of your words. Talk about what you want and not the current happenings in your life. A recent study showed that the *"Average person uses four hundred words or less for eighty percent of everyday conversation"*. Highly competent ladies are always talking what they want. I have met countless ladies who desired to get married, but are saying the wrong things about guys. Some of them will say, *"I don't trust guys". "There are no sincere guys any longer". "Most guys are dubious". "There is no true love anywhere".* These ladies desire to get married but are saying the negative things about guys. And as the law of expectations says 'sooner or later we get just what we expect". They will begin to attract crooked guys to their life. They often find it very difficult to find true and sincere love. Guys will just be hitting and dumping them. Because they always say and believe negative things about guys; they will begin to attract negative guys to their life. If you really want to get married to excellent guys; you must begin to talk good and excellent things about guys. Though, there may be bad and crooked guys out there. But, because you are talking about the kind of guys you want; you will eventually attract the guy that suites your values.

Your choice of words is very powerful in creating your future, that's why you must begin to talk excellently and positively about you future. The spoken words are seed that will sow into our future. Sooner or later, they will soon become a reality. That's why you must begin to speak excellently and positively about your future. Talk about the guys you desire as a spouse. Begin to speak excellent words into your life and you will eventually become an excellent lady.

Be a Master of your Movement
To be a person of self- mastery, you must exercise

absolute control on your movement. You don't go to where you are tolerated; you go to were you are celebrated or appreciated.

That's the only way you are going to become a very respected, organized and competent lady. As a lady that desires to get married, it's not every outing that is worth going. You don't go to dirty outings that will create bad impression about you. If you continue to go to club every day of your life, guys will assume you are a club lady and no excellent guy will want to get along with you.

To really become the lady that guys are eager to marry; you must exercise absolute control over your movement. You don't go to outing that will speak bad or create bad Image of you; you go out to where you are celebrated and appreciated. That's one of the ways to become a master of your life.

Appreciate yourself

Another way to be a master of yourself is to have self-esteem. You must appreciate your beauty, wits and like yourself. Two third of all women and one-third of all men don't like the way they look in the mirror. But if you don't like yourself, how can you be liked by somebody. To become the lady guys are eager to marry, you must appreciate your qualities and uniqueness. As Oscar Wilde, the English poet once said *"To love one self is the beginning of a life long romance"*

If you really want others to appreciate you, then you must as well appreciate yourself. Appreciate you uniqueness;

-       You are remarkable
-       You are beautiful
-       You are special
-       You are excellent

\-   You are gorgeous

When you like yourself, you become a master of your emotion. When you think positively about yourself, you become a very positive person and begin to attract positive things to your life, you will begin to attract positive guys because like begats like.

To like yourself is one of the greatest things you can do to become a very likeable and attractive lady and a master of yourself. That's why you must appreciate yourself because that's the only way you will be appreciated by guys

BE A MASTER OF YOURSELF.

1.   Be an extremely organized lady. Have a sense of control over your taste, desire, emotions, ego, feeling and thinking.

2.   Be a master of your anger. Resolve to always put the emotion of anger under control. Make every effort to always avoid any event that can get you angry.

3.   Be a master of your thinking. Always think in terms of the changes you desired in life and not the immediate happenings in your life. Think about your desired guy. Form the mental picture of your desired spouse.

4.   Be a master of your words. Talk about the changes you desired. Resolve to always say positive and nice things about guys.

5. Be a master of your movement. Do not go to where you are tolerated; always go to where you are appreciated. Make a resolve to exercise absolute control over your movement.

6. Resolve today to always appreciate yourself. Always remember that there is no other person in this world that look or have your exact features. You are unique, pretty, extra-ordinary and special. Always appreciate your self-worth and say positive things about yourself.

10

BE A LADY OF GREAT FAITH IN GOD

He that swims with God never goes to the bottom.
--------------------Polish Proverb.

According to recent studies; the second most prayer request in every church, religious gatherings or conferences is that of marriage partners. Only that of financial success and personal breakthrough is the highest prayer request in all religious gatherings. Millions of ladies these days turn to God seeking the love of their lives especially in the third world countries where the fire of religion is like a fire that can be compared to known in any other continent. Higher percentage of the population of the world now turns to God to seek solutions to their marriage problems. Most ladies go as long as fasting for days seeking spiritual solution to their marriage problems. But, it is very unfortunate most of these ladies never take out time to learn the God laid down principles of marriage. Learning, understanding and applying the God's standard of marriage is all it takes to get attracted to guys for marriage. When you understand and apply this standard and rules, you don't need to pray much to get married to your desired guy. So, ignorant is the main cause of those ladies who keep on praying and fasting for marriage partners but without getting any meaningful and desired results. As God said through Prophet Hosea in the Bible "My people are destroyed for lack of knowledge". (Hosea 4:6). Remember, it says my people. So you can still be going to church and be ignorant of this God's principles of marriage. You can be addicted Christian and still be ignorant of the God's principles of marriage. The foregone chapters of this book showed you the fundamental principles and God's standard for getting married.

This chapter is just to establish the fact that your connection with God will make all the difference in your life. Most ladies who are not believers but learn and cultivate the ideas and principles discussed in the foregone chapters have got married to their desired spouses faster, and easier and without any relationship entanglements . The principles in this book are fundamental things that get you attracted to guys faster than you could ever have imagined possible. The bitter truth is that they are very effective for both Christians and non Christians. If you study the lives of ladies that got married to their desired spouses, you will be amazed that they possessed all the qualities discussed in the foregone chapters irrespective of their religious values.

MARRIAGE IS GOD'S BLESSING

Most ladies keep on crying to God as if God doesn't want them to get married. But if you study Genesis 2: 18-23, you will discover that marriage is God's idea. "And the LORD God said, 'it is not good that the man should be alone. I will make him a helper suitable for him" The first marriage was perfumed by God. So it is His desire for you to get married. But the main reasons most ladies never get married is that they are ignorant of the fundamental principles and standards of marriage. Wrong attitudes are among the major factors hindering most ladies of getting married. That's why this book was well researched to show you why you are not getting married and what you must begin to do to become the most sought-after lady that guys are eager to get married to. Most ladies have cultivated the qualities expounded in the foregone chapters even at an older age, and in no time began to have multiple proposals for marriage.

A wise man once told me *"It gets to a stage in a lady's life that if you give her two options of a husband and a very big fabulous estates "that the lady will probably choose husband"*. It doesn't matter what you have accomplished in any field of life or the amount of wealth you have accumulated. As a lady, if you are not married at a certain stage of your life, there are chances you will not enjoy personal fulfillment. Everything will look ordinary to you. Your life will be boring and you may never become a fulfilled lady. If not for exceptional religious reason, as the case in the Catholic Church. Ladies are defined for marriage and multiplication. But if you are not married, how would you multiply. Tokunbo Ajayi was one of the most intelligent ladies in Nigeria during her lifetime. She was the most effective in the media house. She was one of the best brains in Nigerian Television Authority. She was wealthy, influential, and highly admired by millions of Nigerian viewers but she was not a fulfilled lady. Something was missing in her life. She was not married. This frustration is probably among the factors that led to her untimely death years ago. Marriage is God's blessing to ladies and he cannot deprive that from any lady that desires to get married. But most of those ladies that are finding it difficult to get married are just ignorant of the standards and principles of marriage.

That's why when you learn and cultivate the principles expounded in the foregone chapters, you will automatically become a magnet of great and resourceful guys for marriage.

REBECCA OF THE ANCIENT HISTORY

You probably have read the story of how Rebecca got married to Isaac, the Israelite. As the story was illustrated in Genesis 24: 1- 67, verse 16 says, "And the damsel was very fair to look upon, a virgin, neither had any man known her; and filled her pitcher and came up. And the servant ran to meet her and said, let me, I pray you; drink a little water of your pitcher. And she said, drink my

Lord; and she hastened and emptied her pitcher into the trough and ran again unto the well to draw water, and draw for all his camels. And the man, wondering at her, held his peace, to learn whether the Lord had made his journey prosperous or not. And it came to pass, as the camels had finished drinking, that the man took a golden earring of half a shekel weight, and two bracelets for her hands of ten shekels weight of gold. And said, whose daughter are you. Tell me 1 pray you; is there room in your father's house for us to lodge in. And she said unto him, I am the daughter of Bethuel the son of Micah, whom she bore unto Nahor. She moreover said unto him, we have both straw and fodder enough, and room to lodge in". If you read this story from the beginning, you will discover that Abraham has sent his eldest servant unto his country to look for a wife for Isaac, his covenant son. And when the servant got to the country, decided to stand by the well of water to observe the daughters and ladies that come to draw water. He wanted to marry to Isaac a lady with good and attractive character and the first lady that came to draw water was Rebecca. In other word, Rebecca was working when she experience her marriage destiny. If she has been sleeping at home that day, she wouldn't have married Isaac and another lady would have become Isaac's wife. In those days, females are meant to do the house responsibilities and domestic functions, so Rebecca was working while she met her spouse. As stated in the forgone chapters, to really become the lady that guys are eager to marry; one of the things you must do is to put your career-online. You must be productive and resourceful in life as no guy would want to marry a liability.

Another quality Rebecca possessed and exhibited that day to Abraham's servant was the quality of pleasant, positive and winning character. She had never met this servant before, but despite this, Rebecca demonstrated the quality of absolute respect and was willing to do everything he requested. She didn't only draw water for him but also for all his camels to the extent that Abraham's servant was very amazed at Rebecca's attitudes. *"And the man wondering at her, held his peace".* Genesis 24; 21a. What do you think would have happened if Rebecca has snubbed or ignored Abraham's servant or refused to draw water for him?

The man would have remained by the river until he sees a lady that demonstrated unquestionable and attractive character. Rebecca possessed a unique character that can be compared to none of the ladies of her time. She was a very hardworking, respectful, and enthusiastic lady. She treated Abraham's servant with respect, recognition, politeness, and humility.

As expounded in the foregone chapters of this book, to really become the lady that guys are eager to marry, you must put your character online. Almost 8 out of every 10 ladies of the 21st century would have snubbed, rebuked or ridiculed Abraham's servant, that's why majority of then are finding it extremely difficult to get married. Pleasant character is not a substitute for any lady that desires to get married. An arrogant lady can never and will never be loved. As emphasized in the foregone chapters, one of the ways to command the attention of great guys for marriage is to be a lady of great character. This is what make Rebecca got married to Isaac of the ancient Israel.

GOD MAKES THE DIFFERENCE
To really become the lady that guys are eager to marry, you must abide by God's standards and rules all the days of your life. Let God be your ultimate. The state of your commitment to Jesus the only begotten son of God,

determines the success of your career, relationship, financial and mental life. That's why your relationship with Jesus makes all the difference in your desire to get married. You must understand God's principles for living and abide by his rules and principles. That's the only way you are going to get married faster to your desired guy and become a very effective, powerful and fulfilled lady.

BE A LADY OF GREAT FAITH IN GOD.

1.   Resolve today to make God your ultimate.

2.   Always abide by God's principles and rules for living. Resolve today to make God's word your ultimate.

3.   God makes all the difference in your desire to get married. That's why you must have a working relationship with the Almighty.

4.   Highly fulfilled lady put God first in all they do. You must let God be your ultimate in life.

CONCLUSION

TAKE ACTION TODAY.

Progress is impossible without action.
-------------- Albert Einstein

The principles, ideas, and strategies you have just explored in this book work like magic. That's why you must begin to apply to your life right now all you have learned in this book. That's the only way you are going to become one of the most sought-after ladies that highly resourceful guys are eager to marry. If you are one of those ladies that are finding it difficult to get married; the good thing you can do now is to take the personal inventory of yourself, admit your personal faults and begin to correct those wrong attitudes that have hindered you from getting married over the years. You must admit your faults and be willing to change rather than complaining, murmuring, or blaming yourself, others or your circumstances for your predicaments. As Albert Einstein, one of the most intelligent men who ever lived said, "Once we accept our limits, we go beyond them". This book is an eye-opener, that shows you your wrong doing, poor attitudes and manners that have stopped you from getting married. It also shows the kinds of attitudes, characters and qualities you need to cultivate to get married faster and quicker to your desired guy. Thousands of ladies have cultivated the qualities expounded in this book and got married to their desired guys faster than their widest imaginations. It doesn't matter your age or how long you have been diligently seeking the love of your life; once you cultivate and begin to exhibit the qualities you have just explored in this book; you will become a magnet of guys. Once you begin to exhibit these qualities to people; within a matter of weeks, months or a short period, guys will begin to woo, chase and persuade you for marriage.

As a lady; one of the greatest frustrations you can ever experience in life is to get married to the guy that doesn't meet your standards, suite your values or you don't really love from your heart. Most ladies do this out of frustration. I recently heard of a lady; a Barrister by profession who said she's ready to marry any man that propose to her for marriage. This lady is frustrated because she has had it very difficult despite her lucrative career to get married.

The principles you have just explored in this book will save you from having this kind of bitter experience or from getting married to a guy that doesn't meet your standard or make you a fulfilled lady.
Here again are the top ten qualities you must cultivate to get married to your desired guy
faster in weeks and months ahead.

1.   BE A LADY OF GREAT CHARACTER;
there is no substitute for unquestionable character for any lady that will attract great guys for marriage. Most 21st century guys are willing to substitute outstanding physical qualities to outstanding character. That's why you must put your character online to become a magnet of great, resourceful and effective guys for marriage.

2.   BE A LADY OF GREAT DREAMS;

highly ambitious, goal-oriented and enthusiastic ladies are always commanders of men attention for marriage. When you have a clear sense of purpose, sense of meaning, sense of direction, and sense of goals towards a glorious future; you will become the magnet of highly ambitious guys for marriage. When you are extremely goal-driven and highly resourceful lady; highly ambitious guys will perceive that quality in you and be willing to spend the rest of their lives with you knowing fully well that both of you will be better-off as a couple.

3. BE A RESOURCEFUL AND PRODUCTIVE LADY;

Gone are the days when men were willing to shoulder the total responsibility of marriage. Now, the 21st century guys are looking out for highly resourceful and productive ladies that will complement their efforts in marriage. They want ladies that will play a part in the home responsibilities. After all, *two are always better than one*. No guy wants to have a liability as a spouse, most guys want to marry an asset and a productive lady. To really become the lady that guys are eager to marry; you must be resourceful and productive in life.

4. BE A MASTER OF DRESSING;

Intelligent dressing sense enhances your ability to get married. As a lady, the ability to always dress attractively in a way that suites every occasion and outing is one of the greatest things you can ever do to command the attention of guys for marriage. And you should always remember that to dress attractively doesn't mean to dress seductively or lavish all your income on buying wears. You must have a sense of dressing. You must have a sense of control on how you dress because every of your dressing sends out a telling statement to others about you. You must always dress uniquely, attractively and nicely.

5.   BE AN INTELLIGENT LADY;

Highly intelligent lady are among the greatest asset on earth. That's why they always command attention of highly competent guys for marriage. But, it is very unfortunate that it's only ten of every a hundred of 21st century ladies that are intelligent. If you are very intelligent in doing things, you will command the attention of guys for marriage. That's why you must begin to make every effort to sharpen your intelligence, improve your knowledge and enhance your skills. That's one of the ways to command great attention among guys.

6.   BE A CHEERFUL LADY;

hundreds of studies have ascertained the fact that cheerful, happy and positive ladies can easily influence men to their cause than frowning ones. That's why highly cheerful and enthusiastic ladies always get things done faster, influence guys easier, get their request approved quicker, and receive more privileges, respect and attention from guys than the ladies that are of the habit of frowning. Most guys can displease themselves to please a lady that exhibits the quality of cheerfulness and smiles to them in any life dealing. Cheerful ladies are great commander of great attention from guys. That's why you must cultivate these remarkable qualities to attract great guys for marriage.

7.   BE A LADY OF PLEASANT PERSONALITY;

The ability to always treat people with utmost respect, sincerity, recognition and humility is perhaps some of the greatest qualities you can ever possess to command the attention of guys for marriage. *An arrogant lady can never be loved.* It is against the marriage system. Guys can easily be pissed-off by a proud and rude lady. The quality of submission is not a substitute in your desire to get married. That's why you must always be respectful and treat everyone with utmost recognition, honesty and respect. That's the only way you will become the favourite of responsible guys for marriage.

8.   BE A HEALTHY LADY;

Health is the greatest quality of human. A healthy lady will always attract a healthy relationship that will lead to healthy marriage. You must make every effort to be a very healthy lady. Make a commitment today to always involve in the activities that will improve the quality of your health. Learn the healthy skills. Think healthy, associate with healthy people and make your environment very healthy. Become an extremely healthy lady and you will attract healthy guys for marriage.

9.   BE A MASTER OF YOURSELF;
To really command the attention of great and highly resourceful guys for marriage, you must have a sense of control, sense of discipline, sense of purpose, sense of association, sense of goals

nd cultivate the quality of self-mastery. A life
ithout control is heading for a ruin. When
ou are master of your emotion, thinking, anger, and
ords; you will become a very organized, competent,
nd effective lady and eventually command the attention
f great guys for marriage.

). BE A LADY OF GREAT FAITH IN GOD;
his is the foundation for a successful and
ulfilled life. You must let God be your
ltimate. As a lady aspiring to get married; you must
nderstand God's principles and standard for marriage
nd live by those standards all the days of your life. You
ust have an excellent relationship with God; the
mighty. You must have a working relationship with
esus; our Lord. That's the best relationship you can ever
evelop to become a very successful, powerful and
ulfilled lady.

ou have just explored perhaps the most comprehensive
nd powerful ideas, principles and strategies in history
r getting married faster to the guy that meets your
andards, suites your values and makes you powerful
nd fulfilled lady. These are the secrets known only to
ighly fulfilled ladies that are enjoying excellent
arriages today.

/hen you learn, cultivate, imbibe, exhibit and make
ese qualities part and parcel of your life; you get your
fe loosed for greater accomplishments and marriage
ulfillments. You will attract great guys for marriage, get
arried to your desired guys and experience a
emorable, honourable and fulfilled marriage.

othing can stop you! Get loosed and get married to
our desired spouse.
ood Luck!

FESTUS A TOKS

AUTHOR - SPEAKER - CONSULTANT.

Festus A Toks is one of the most knowledgeab
authorities today on the subjects of huma
relationships and personal development. His idea
insights, and training materials have been sough
after by thousands of people for effective a1
fulfilled life.

Festus has authored several books on the subjects
human relationship, success-system and persona
effectiveness which includes;

1.   Towards Academic Excellence.
   2. Winning Strategies.
   3. Courtship, Sex and singles.
   4. The laws of Excellence Achievement.
   5. Unlimited Achievement and
   6. Success Qualities.

For more information, visit; www.festytoks.com.
Register for a free subscription to one or more
Festy's powerful insights on Personal Success, Tin
Management, Relationship Success, Marriag
Fulfillment and Financial Mastery.
To book Festus as a conference speaker, contact;

Festus Toks International,
7, Sonibare Street Isolo,
Lagos, Nigeria.
Tel; +234-8027589528.
www.festytoks.com.

ABOUT THE AUTHOR

Festus A Toks, a Consultant, Multi-gifted Author, Relationships strategists and Entrepreneur is the CEO of Festus Toks International; a human, corporate and leadership resource development organization; dedicated to helping people discover, develop, deplore and fully utilized their personal potentials, abilities and powers to excellence performance and maximum achievement.

Festus is an avid student of Psychology, relationships, leadership, management, personal-development, history, economics, politics, marriage and religion. His insights, ideas and training materials have been commended by Governments, policy-makers, political thinkers and adopted by thousands of people for effective performance.

Festus believes that each person has unlimited and extra-ordinary personal-powers and potentials to live an excellence and remarkable life and he's dedicated to make anybody that comes his way live the life of a masterpiece.

Festus, an authority on personal-effectiveness, self-development and corporate-excellence is one of the leading thinkers of the 21st century philosophers and writers. His powerful, life-strengthen insights, ideas and inspiration has made a remarkable and tremendous impact in the lives of thousands of people.

Festus resides in Abuja, Nigeria